COLLEGE
KNOWLEDGE
for the Jewish Student

101 Tips

DAVID SCHOEM

THE UNIVERSITY OF MICHIGAN PRESS
Ann Arbor

For My Jewish Students

ISBN: 978-0-472-03430-7

2013   2012   2011   2010   4   3   2   1

Library of Congress Cataloging-in-Publication Data

Schoem, David Louis.
     College knowledge for the Jewish student : 101 tips / David
Schoem.
          p. cm.
     ISBN 978-0-472-03430-7   (pbk. : alk. paper)
     1.   Jewish college students–Life skills guides.   2.   College
student orientation.   I.   Title.
   LB3613.J4S44 2010
   378.1'9829924073–dc22   2010021415

Preface

The first year of college is an exhilarating experience for Jewish students. It is a year when the rush of adrenaline alone is enough to carry a student forward on most days. Time moves in the extreme, as the excitement of much greater freedom and independence, stimulating courses, and new friends makes everything speed by.

Most students arrive at college without having given thought to their personal and educational goals or how to best take advantage of the rich resources that their college offers. There is so much attention on the business of "getting into college" that too few students and their families take the time necessary to consider how to make the most of the college experience itself. It saddens me to hear students in their junior or senior years of college first begin to realize the opportunity that college holds for them and how they wished they had spent their first years differently. I hope this book will provide more students and their families with the resources and incentive to take the time prior to the start of college and during the first year of college to reflect on the college experience.

Higher education has served as an intellectual and social haven for Jews. Even so, for each individual Jewish student who enters college, it is critical that he or she come intellectually, emotionally, and spiritually prepared for the academic and social experiences that await. College is a qualitatively different experience than high school, and students' expectations need to be set appropriately. The transition from high school to college is so significant that it can be difficult for most without some preparation. The most successful college students I have known have modeled the advice that follows in this book.

I encourage Jewish students reading this book who will be entering college or who are already in their first year of college to carry these ideas with you to help insure that your transition goes well. Read the tips, digest them, and keep them close by for the many moments when you may need some direction and support. Then brace yourself for the ride of a lifetime—the first year of college.

Every tip and vignette in this book has for me brought up memories of the many wonderful Jewish students I have taught and counseled throughout my career. Each tip and vignette reflects a composite of enlightening experiences and conversations with multiple Jewish students with whom I have worked. It has made the writing of this book very special in a way that is quite different from other books I have authored and edited.

As I have written this book, I have made every attempt to consider the experiences at all types of post-secondary institutions. Given my scholarly work in the higher education field and my travels to small liberal arts colleges, large research universities, and everything in-between, I am confident that the tips presented here apply across institutional types. However, because I have been a faculty member at the University of Michigan for many years, I recognize that I may necessarily be influenced a bit by college life at the large public research university and therefore advise the reader that, on occasion, some tips and vignettes may seem a closer fit for some settings than others.

I feel so fortunate, particularly as a first-generation Jewish college student, to have had the schooling and subsequent scholarly profession that have allowed me to learn, study, and teach throughout my life. I have written and taught about Jewish identity, the American Jewish community, Jewish education, and relations between the American

Jewish community and other racial, religious, and ethnic groups. My University of Michigan sociology courses on Jewish Identity and the Sociology of the American Jewish Community have been among my favorites. I remain in touch with many of my students from those classes, including those who met their Jewish partner in class and subsequently married. All the while I have had the opportunity to put theory into practice, working directly with thousands of intellectually creative, dynamic, and caring college students.

I have been in one or another teaching role since I led Junior Congregation services and tutored Bar/Bat Mitzvah students as a teenager in Philadelphia at Har Zion Temple where my father served for many years as executive director. For many summers I was a camper and then counselor at Camp Ramah; taught in an afternoon Hebrew School; worked as a day-care, nursery school, and elementary school teacher's assistant at alternative and traditional schools both here in the United States and in the British Infant Schools; and earned a secondary school teaching certificate. I fondly recall my daily dinners as a student at the kosher kitchen table at Hillel at the University of Michigan and the opportunity to take a year of independent study in Israel during college. My Ph.D. dissertation, a study of how the Jewish community passes on its culture and traditions in pluralistic America by examining Jewish afternoon schools of various denominations, was named the most outstanding dissertation on Jewish Education, 1970-80, from the Institute of Contemporary Jewry at the Hebrew University of Jerusalem and later revised and published as a book, entitled *Ethnic Survival in America: An Ethnography of a Jewish Afternoon School.*

I am also a scholar, professor, and administrator in higher education and of intergroup relations, focusing on social scientific theory and practice about undergraduate education, K-12 education, social identity, diversity and intergroup dialogue, civic engagement, community, deliberative democracy, and social change. This book, while clearly written for an educated but non-academic audience, is carefully grounded in the broad scholarship of higher education research and my own extensive practice in the field.

I have spent most of my career working in the area of undergraduate education at the University of Michigan, and I have also given talks, led seminars, and offered consultations and workshops for faculty at more than fifty small and large, private and public, urban and rural, regional and elite colleges and universities. Subsequent to my own education at the University of Michigan, Harvard University, and the University of California at Berkeley, I have been a professor, dean, and vice president for academic affairs and student affairs. I am currently director of the Michigan Community Scholars Program and a member of the faculty of the Sociology and Judaic Studies Departments. In these various roles, I have been involved in almost all aspects of undergraduate education at one time or another, from curriculum committees to diversity and undergraduate initiatives to advisory boards on student life, admissions, wellness, etc. I have both written about and developed initiatives on learning communities, first-year seminars, and intergroup dialogues, among many other topics. I have written extensively about many aspects of higher education and worked closely with inspiring colleagues at colleges and national higher education organizations across the nation who have dedicated their lives to improving undergraduate education in the United States.

Much of my time, commitment, and effort, however, have gone to working directly with undergraduate students, as their teacher, advisor, program director, mentor, and friend. I have benefited enormously from my relationships with my students, growing and learning from each outstanding individual I have met. I hope this book in some small way expresses my gratitude for all that they have given to me.

Acknowledgments

For many years I have received requests to provide tips for college success to incoming college students at recruitment events and orientations. Faculty and college administrators from around the country would call me for advice for their children and grandchildren who were about to enter college as undergraduates. My Jewish friends started to send their children to college and would approach me with these same questions.

Given these experiences and my own immersion in the scholarship of higher education, the tips for this book have come quickly and easily. As I've written this book, I have received many suggestions from friends, parents, and respected colleagues. I have also relied on my many exceptional Jewish students—too many to mention here, but you know who you are—as one of the best sources for grounding the tips in reality.

I am indebted to Kelly Sippell and Phil Pochoda of the University of Michigan Press for inviting me to write this book. While it builds on the success of my earlier book, *College Knowledge: 101 Tips*, they understood that there were unique issues facing Jewish college students and their families that would be best served by a book addressing their specific concerns.

This is my fourth book with the University of Michigan Press, including *Inside Separate Worlds: Life Stories of Young Blacks, Jews, and*

Latinos; Intergroup Dialogue: Deliberative Democracy in School, College, Community, and Workplace; and the earlier *College Knowledge: 101 Tips* book. Throughout the years, the editors and staff at UM Press, especially Mary Erwin, Christina Milton, and Mary Bisbee-Beek, have always been as helpful as possible.

I want to thank my early mentors in Jewish life, including Elliot Dorff, Ron Wolfson, Isa Aron, Harlene Appelman, Arnie Dashefsky, Harold Himelfarb, Edy Rauch, Barry Chazan, Shelly Dorph, Stuart Kelman, Hy Pomerantz, Neil Newman, Judah Pilch, and Abraham Gannes as well as my many Judaic Studies colleagues and friends in the Jewish community in Ann Arbor and beyond. Special thanks to Leslie Meyers. My lifelong friends, Edward "Yitze" Miller, Josh Wall, and Allen Weinstock, as well as Nomi Davidson, Janet Landay, Isa Goldfarb, and Hanna Cohn, have shared our Jewish lives and family's lives since childhood.

In higher education, I owe many thanks to mentors and colleagues, including Jim Robertson, Don Oliver, John Ogbu, Sheila Walker, Don Brown, Harold Shapiro, Jim Crowfoot, Pat Gurin, Mark Chesler, Terry Joiner, Caryn McTighe Musil, Nancy Thomas, Jean MacGregor, Emily Lardner, Gillies Malnarich, Ximena Zuniga, and Beverly Tatum. My UM faculty men's group on religious exploration, including George Cooper, Joe Galura, Luis Sfeir-Younis, Charles Behling, Jim Crowfoot, and Ed St. John, have been a great support in recent years. All of my colleagues at Michigan, especially through the Michigan Community Scholars Program, including Wendy Woods, Rosa Maria Cabello, Amanda Hooper, Emily Yee, Kate Gallup, and Jaimie Philip, and at colleges and national associations across the country have helped me understand what it takes to mentor and support undergraduates in their search for fulfillment, meaning, and success.

Finally, I wish to again thank my loving family for bearing with me through yet another intensive writing experience on this, my eighth

ACKNOWLEDGMENTS

book. Karyn, Adina, and Shana offer constant encouragement and humor, joking and asking about the latest tip. Karyn's support and love has been steadfast as we soon look forward to our 28th anniversary. Adina and Shana have successfully "tip"-toed through college and onto graduate studies and beyond. A recent homemade Father's Day card declared, "Tip 101: A family who loves you with all their hearts!" The truth, however, is that these days I increasingly find myself listening intently to their ideas and advice in place of offering my own. I guess that's Tip 102: Listen to your children.

Contents

3. Milk and Honey: Getting the Most out of College   51

6. Life on Campus for Jewish Students   134

The Ten Commandments for College Success and Happiness

1 Believe in Your (Jewish) Self

As a Jew, you are a member of the "People of the Book." Your parents and grandparents hold high expectations for you in college and in life. Your synagogue or temple has honored you and put you on a pedestal for your high school accomplishments. Your peers are bright, have high aspirations for college, and all seem to have done well throughout their schooling. Your siblings have been very successful at college. It's all great, right?

But talk about pressure!! OK, take a deep breath and relax. Everything is going to work out just fine.

I can't overstate the importance of maintaining your self-confidence at college. You are a bright, capable person, and if you have good study habits and the desire to succeed, you will do just that at each and every college that offered you admission. Know that this is true, remind yourself daily, and never question your intellectual abilities.

There is a mind game that gets played out at every college regardless of its guidebook ranking. Very simply, students worry that they're not up to the college's or their family's standard. Unfortunately, colleges do very little to allay such fears. First-year students look at their peers in the residence hall cafeteria, at the college convocation, or at the first lecture or seminar and worry that they're just not as smart as the other students.

Many students, when they are speaking openly to me, wonder aloud whether the college admissions office made a mistake in admitting them. Deep down in a vulnerable place inside them, they imagine that if the college admissions office had truly read their applications carefully, they would not have been deserving of admission. After all, with so many other smart students in their school and now sitting with them in college, how could they have been fully competitive and worthy of admission?

I experienced this same fear when I attended college many years ago. Sure, I was a good student in high school, but I worried that I would be found out once I got to college. Maybe the admissions office accidentally put my application in the wrong pile and sent me the wrong letter. I wondered whether colleges ever send out "so sorry" letters retracting admissions to students like me.

Of course this is all silliness. And if such a notion should ever come over you, just let go of it immediately. College admissions offices know what they're doing. The truth is that colleges receive applications from so many outstanding students that they must reject hundreds, even thousands, of qualified students. So, clearly, everyone who is admitted is fully capable of doing outstanding work. The key is discovering what your interests are, finding your own identity, meeting good students and faculty, and developing good study skills.

When you hear others talk about all the smart kids at college, know that they're talking about you. SAT/ACT scores? Once you're in college, no one cares about those exams and what your score was. Your high school GPA? Forget it. After the first few weeks of college, high school will seem like years in the past. No one is interested. What faculty members and the other students will be interested in is you—in your ideas, your interests, what you care about, what classes you are taking, papers you are writing, books you are reading, and what you hope to accomplish in your life.

When I first entered high school in ninth grade with a class of 1,500 other students, our principal gave a welcoming speech to us in our huge high school auditorium. He told us to look at the student sitting next to us on our right and then to turn and look at the student sitting next to us on our left. Then he told us that in four years, at the end of twelfth grade, one of the three of us would not be there for graduation. I remember that sorry speech and its negative message all too well.

But unlike my high school principal's advice, you should approach your college education with full confidence that you will graduate in four years. And your expectation should be not just that you will graduate, but that you will excel. In college you will begin the path of realizing your academic, professional, and personal dreams.

Right now, take out a piece of paper and write "I know I am smart. I know I can do well in college. I believe in myself and in my academic abilities. I will achieve to the top of my ability. I will accomplish great things." Put this paper in a secret place. Read it to yourself as often as you need. Self-confidence is your first insurance policy for success in college.

2 Learn to Be a College Student: You're Not in High School Anymore

College is an entirely different universe than high school, and your job is to explore that new universe as you move on to the rest of your life. College is not just different; it is a far richer, more substantive, and deeper learning environment than high school. It's important to come to college personally and mentally prepared and with the right expectations for your college experience and growth as a young adult. Get ready to immerse yourself in an entirely different type and quality of learning.

The worst mistake you can make is to imagine that college is like high school. That's a nightmarish vision. Think about it. Only if you had failed twelfth grade would you still be in high school. Fortunately, you were a very successful high school student, and your reward and opportunity is to go on to the great educational adventure that is college. Don't waste the next four years of your life repeating your high school experience.

At the end of four years of high school, you, along with the other best-educated students in the country, typically know five areas of intellectual thought, including math, science, English, U.S. history, and a second language. To be certain, these are important fields. But a world of ideas awaits you when you enter college.

Most colleges, in their effort to help guide you in the process of broadening your intellectual horizons, require you to take a series of required courses in various disciplinary areas. Unfortunately, too many students embrace these requirements in the old high school mold. They organize their course selection for their first year of college in a manner that will help them "get the requirements out of the way." Please don't approach your first year of college as yet another year of ugly requirements, forcing you to delay for yet another year the excitement of learning that awaits you.

What steps can you take in your first year to embrace the best that college has to offer? First, take at least one first-year seminar. In a first-year seminar, you will sit in a class of between twelve and twenty students with a faculty member who loves to teach undergraduates, exploring with other bright students a field in which you all have an interest. Most important, you will build a small community of interested learners, students, and faculty, meeting a few times each week to question, challenge, analyze, and think about ideas that are important to you and the world around you. The small seminar setting is the epitome of the college experience with active and engaged learners in a scholarly community of faculty and students.

Second, take courses with good teachers. Regardless of how interested you are in any given course content or course description, you are better off following good teachers. With good teachers you will be inspired, you will be engaged, you will build a relationship, and you will want to do good work and to learn beyond the limits of the course syllabus.

Third, try out a new idea. It is the very essence of college. College is a place filled with people who think about ideas. This is a chance you must not miss out on, a chance to give voice to all your ideas—the wondrous ones, the ones that will some day save lives, the inventive ones, and also those that are half-baked, barely formed, and that on face value seem almost ridiculous. Trying out an idea is so exciting in college because there is a community of faculty and friends who will take you seriously and listen and respond to you.

Fourth, try out a new field of study that you've never considered before. Take a course in some field in which you know very little or even nothing. Yes, there's some risk here. You might find out you're not particularly interested in this field. But if you consider how many years you've been studying the same old topic over and over again without any choice, as if there were only a handful of topics in the world to study, this is a pretty small risk. And the benefits could be enormous. Take some intellectual risks, please!

Fifth, try out your Jewish identity as an independent young adult. Explore what being Jewish means to you, unencumbered by parental or communal obligations to practice and believe in one or another particular way. Examine the many different Jewish approaches to prayer, faith, holiness, personal behavior, social justice, God, values, relationships, and Israel. Choose for yourself what this identity means for you and how, or in some cases even whether, you want to embrace and embody it.

Sixth, try out a new career. No, most of you don't have to start looking for full-time work just yet. But imagine what life will be like for you if you choose to be an artist, a teacher, a CEO, a writer, a scientist, an engineer, a doctor, a survey researcher, an interpreter, a community organizer, or a forest ranger. Many students come to college thinking that their career choices are limited to medicine, law, engineering, and business. Don't think in that limiting way; your career choices are wide open.

Seventh, try out a new friend. High school friendships can be comforting and supportive as you enter an entirely new environment, but if you want to move on with your life and meet the world, then college is precisely the time to assert yourself, make new friends, and pursue your own identity. Students in your college will come from a variety of racial, ethnic, class, religious, sexual orientation, geographic, and national backgrounds, and you should meet these people.

Eighth, try out a new perspective. You might change your perspective or reaffirm your current viewpoint, but in doing so you will most definitely begin to take responsibility for thinking critically and holding your own views. And, hopefully, you'll begin to see the world beyond factoids and sound bites and understand the complexities of issues. See the world from a point of view of someone who has different interests, comes from a different part of the country or world, or is of a different gender or religion.

3   Get to Know Faculty

Getting to know faculty at your college must be one of your top priorities. It will make your college experience.

Don't consider yourself an A student if you don't know at least one professor well enough to ask a question, ask for advice, discuss some academic topic, and request a letter of recommendation. You haven't completed your college education yet. And if you know one or more faculty well and you're not an A or B student, you have greatly increased the chances that you will walk at graduation in four years alongside your peers. It is well known that students who succeed in college have good relationships with one or more faculty members.

One way to think about faculty is that they are brilliant scholars, cutting-edge researchers, inspiring teachers, first-rate authors, and consultants to leaders in every imaginable field around the globe. For most first-year students, that's a surefire intimidating mind-set that will permanently keep you 50 yards away from the nearest faculty member in sight.

I suggest you step back from that approach for a moment. Try imagining your professor or instructor as a parent, a child, or a sibling. A professor or instructor is someone who likes to spend much of his or her day reading, creating, thinking, discovering, experimenting, writing, and engaging in interesting discussions with smart people just like you.

Faculty are regular people, just like you. Faculty have their good points and their flaws. They have their likes and dislikes. They worry about money, health, and taxes; watch sports; take an interest in politics; have close friends; and sometimes are in good, friendly moods but on other days are the opposite. What distinguishes faculty from others, however, is their interest in ideas as a lifelong pursuit.

This characteristic of faculty makes getting to know them such a special and unique opportunity. You get to spend four years in their environment—in their classes, their labs, their offices, their lecture halls, their campus hangouts—during which time your primary purpose is to pursue ideas and the intellectual life. It's in this sense that college is so different from high school. These faculty people don't just come to work to teach you. They live and breathe their intellectual work 24 hours a day, and they're delighted to have you join them in their journey during your short stay in their environment. Don't miss out!

So how do you meet a faculty member? The best approach is to meet them in the classroom by taking a small enough class or seminar that personal relationships naturally develop. You see your instructors a few times a week in class, they debate ideas with you, and they read your papers and write back to you with insightful comments. You'll likely feel comfortable meeting with them after class or during office hours.

But because many of your classes won't be small seminars, it's important to take advantage of other approaches to meet faculty. Go up to the faculty member after class and follow up on a question or idea that was raised in class. Do the same during office hours. Check to see if there are any opportunities to be a research assistant for a faculty member. Some colleges have mentor programs to provide structure for meeting faculty. Invite an instructor to eat lunch with you in your residence hall, at a student union cafeteria, or at a local sandwich shop. Ask a professor if he or she would be willing to speak at a meeting of some organization you're a part of. Join a college committee that includes students as another way to meet and talk with faculty.

And if you are fortunate enough to have a professor or instructor who invites your class over to his or her house for dinner, by all means, GO! No excuses are acceptable. Don't assume you will have this opportunity again in college. As one very bright student told me recently, if your faculty member invites you to *anything,* GO!

What should you say to your professors when you do decide you're ready to talk with them? Ask them about themselves, about what they do, and about how they got interested in their field. Ask them what they're working on now and whether it is a new research project, a journal article, a book, a community project, or a conference presentation. Tell them about a book you're reading or something you've been wondering about related to your class. Feel free to talk about any topic related directly or indirectly to the class. Tell them about your own intellectual and social interests and about your professional goals. All of these questions and topics will lead to enriching conversations and friendships that you will maintain throughout college and, in many cases, well beyond.

Finally, you will want to know a professor or instructor well enough that you can ask that person for a recommendation letter. In most cases, you will be rewarded with such kind words in the letter that you'll find yourself thrilled at how proud the academic world is of your intellectual pursuits and accomplishments.

DANIEL WISEMAN—*"Tutoring Is for A Students."*

Daniel Wiseman is taking the pre-business curricular track. He has always known that he would be good in business, and his parents have always encouraged and assumed that this would be his career. In high school his dad set up summer internships for him in business, and Daniel has loved following the stock market in the daily newspaper.

Daniel started off his first semester with a course load that included calculus and economics. The first few weeks of math class were mostly review from high school, and Daniel felt very confident about his academic preparation and performance. He needed only to study a couple nights a week to stay on pace with the course.

All of a sudden, or so it seemed, the course picked up steam. The material the professor began to cover was all new to Daniel, and the problem sets were quite difficult. And there were so many of them! Daniel was used to just studying a few hours per week on each subject, and he didn't have the study habits in place to put in sufficient time to keep up. Within two weeks time with the new material, Daniel realized that he was falling way behind and his first major test was coming up the next week.

Daniel had always been an A student. He had never received lower than a B in high school. Yet, on his first test, Daniel got a C-, having missed all the questions testing the material he had not already learned in high school. Daniel was embarrassed to say anything to anyone about getting help because he never had to seek help in high school. In fact, he had been a math tutor in high school. Daniel began to worry that all his plans for a career in business were not going to be realized.

After the first test, Daniel couldn't help but observe that many other students were upset about their grades. Although people were grousing about the professor and how she should have explained the material better, a few students mentioned that they were going to participate in study groups. They invited Daniel to join them, and grudgingly he agreed.

When Daniel attended his first study group session, he recognized that there were all levels of students present. He didn't think some of the students were so smart, but he also knew that others were the absolute stars of the class and had received A grades on the exam. He was surprised to see such a mix of students. During the study session, a number of students spoke of meeting the professor during office hours to get help on certain questions. Others mentioned that they were also going to the math department's "math lab" for extra assistance.

All of this was entirely new to Daniel. Yes, he had read about the math lab in the course syllabus. And, yes, he knew his teacher consistently invited students to office hours. But Daniel had always thought that going for help was not for people like him. He decided to give it a try because he knew he had to do better on his exams.

Daniel started taking advantage of all of these resources—office hours, math lab, and the study group. It wasn't as bad as he thought, and no one stigmatized him for asking for help. In fact, he got lots of positive feedback from his friends and parents for his effort and interest. He found that he was starting to pick up the new material and had a group of friends who shared his struggle. Daniel's confidence and determination got a big boost from all of this work, he began to put in many additional hours studying, and he again started to feel that he could achieve his goals. Next exam, Daniel got an A, and on his final he got an A–.

4 Get Involved and Be Engaged

It is highly important to your success in college that you feel attached to your college and are involved in campus life. Not only is it important for your mental and emotional well-being, but it is also a central ingredient for your academic success. Students who feel a connection to their college are much more likely to do well there, to go on to graduate, and to report having had positive college experiences.

It's probably easier at first glance to understand the importance of being involved if you are attending a large public university. At a large university, there may be 15,000, 20,000, 35,000, or even 40,000 or more students on campus. Coming from a high school and perhaps a neighborhood in which it seemed just about everyone knew, admired, and cared about you, you may naturally feel isolated and lonely. How will you ever stand out and be noticed as the unique and special individual that you are?

As a student who has purposely chosen a small liberal arts college, you may anticipate that you've already addressed this concern by your selection of a small college. But in a surprising way, choosing a smaller college can produce some feelings that are similar to those of your peers at larger universities. After all, if you find yourself feeling lonely and homesick at a small college, it's likely that you'll attribute these feelings as being your own doing rather than the fault of the college's size or impersonal atmosphere. At your college, everyone appears to be nice and interested in each individual, and students know one another, yet you are feeling like you're an outsider, on the periphery.

What to do? The simple answer is to get involved. And by getting involved, you may want to attempt a variety of strategies, reaching beyond those that worked for you in high school. Especially if you are attending college with friends from high school, you should definitely explore—on your own—getting involved in campus activities, events, and organizations.

Most colleges have academic structures whose very purpose is to create smaller, more personal, learning environments. One popular structure is called "learning communities." Typically, these programs have the best teachers in the university. They may be academic programs located in the residence hall where you live, or they may be organized as two or more courses together, not associated with any housing situation.

In addition, many colleges today have programs for undergraduates to participate in research with faculty. While this may sound intimidating to a new college student, it is, in fact, one of the best ways to get to know (and be known by) faculty and students on a personal basis.

Almost every college has a Hillel, Chabad House, or other Jewish organization to welcome you to school. There are Jewish student organizations with a focus on Jewish religious, cultural, and Israel-centered activities, and often a building or home that is a comfortable place to hang out. Try attending a Friday evening Shabbat dinner or the first Jewish student mass meeting, or try going to services for the High Holidays in the first weeks of college. Whether your Jewish identity is central or peripheral to you and whether you are religiously observant or not, you are likely to meet some other students and adult leaders who share similar interests with you and will be eager to get to know you and help you feel comfortable and connected at college.

Community service learning is another organized feature on most campuses, and a growing number of campuses are now offering course-based intergroup dialogues. These courses bring students together from two or more social identity groups to talk openly and frankly about difficult issues between groups.

Then there are the myriad campus organizations. Every college has student organizations to suit your interests in politics, sports, media, art, music and theater, writing, race and ethnicity, religion, and so on. Academic departments often have student clubs for those who want to pursue in more depth their interest in chemistry, genetics, creative writing, language, politics, or whatever.

In addition to the option of getting involved in an organization, opportunities exist every day on campus and off to attend lectures, concerts, or plays; to participate in intramural sports or pick-up games; and to do all kinds of other things. Read the student newspaper, check the postings on campus bulletin boards and telephone poles, visit the websites of campus organizations, and find an event to get you out of your room into the residence hall and out into the campus community.

Some students will want to do more than attend events or participate in organizations. There are numerous opportunities to become student leaders on campus in existing organizations or academic clubs, and students can even set up their own organizations. Workshops and retreats are offered to give students experience and skills in leadership, and there are all kinds of networks of student leaders.

These wonderful opportunities will allow you to feel connected intellectually and socially to college life. And be sure not to let yourself feel overwhelmed. Take things slowly, make your choices carefully, and manage your time well. You will have four—or more—years to try out these academic and social options, so don't rush to get all of this done in the first few weeks of college.

5 Expand Your Comfort Zone and Change the World

The first days of college can be rather intimidating socially. After four or more years with the same group of friends, having established a reputation among your peers and teachers, having been a leader in school and community groups, and having been recognized as a very special person, you now have to start all over. Or so it seems at the time. At this anxiety-filled moment, many students are inclined to withdraw to what feels most comfortable, which is their homogeneous, high school friendship circle.

High school friends are good and fine, but it's a mistake to retreat to them just for security. It's a mistake because now you are in college and you don't have to repeat your high school experience. In college you should be experiencing new friends, new ideas, and new worlds.

College truly is the time for you to think beyond yourself and meet the world from which you've been secluded for most of your life. It's like being sent to your room for the first 18 years of life. Most entering college students have led very narrow, protected, and sheltered social lives.

Most college students come from neighborhoods and schools that are highly segregated by race, religion, and class. While this is true for all groups of students, research shows it is particularly true of white students. If you retreat to the comfort zone of your high school days, it's as if you are locking yourself in your room and imposing a strict curfew on yourself.

In college you have the opportunity to meet a whole range of new people with different backgrounds and different ideas from yours. They may see the world through very different lenses. Get to know how to wear their lenses in addition to your own. It will sharpen your vision as you begin to imagine yourself helping to better the world.

Even within the Jewish community, it is still the exception that Jewish students who come from orthodox, conservative, or reform backgrounds have spent much, if any time at all, with their peers from these other denominations. The same is true for Jews of different economic and racial backgrounds. It will be a revelation to you to learn firsthand from other Jews who have grown up with very different ideas and experiences.

Look around your classroom. There are 25 very interesting and smart people there. Look at the faces in your cafeteria. There are 250 interesting and smart people there. Get to know these people. Each one has an interesting and inspiring life story that you should hear. And you should hear their stories not because your life story is not exemplary or because you should model any one of them, but rather because all these people should be an important part of your college education. Talk to your college peers. Learn about their experiences and ideas. Check out your own ideas with them. See what they think.

If you come from a big city, you will have the opportunity to meet people from small or rural towns. In what ways do they view politics and interpret books differently or the same as you do? If you come from a liberal background, talk to a student whose parents are conservative and find out what that person's perspective is. If you are a student who has to work 20 hours a week just to make tuition payments, get to know someone whose family can afford to fly that student home on weekends. What things do you have in common, and in what ways are your worlds so different that it takes a special effort to speak a common language? Consider taking a friend to attend a cultural or religious event from your background and then go to a cultural or religious event from your friend's background.

Research tells us that students in diverse classrooms learn more deeply and understand issues in a more complex fashion. Students who have embraced the diversity of their colleges are better prepared for participating in a diverse workforce, negotiating contracts with people from different backgrounds, and supervising or being supervised by a wide range of people. Experiencing diversity provides needed expertise for future doctors treating their patients, government leaders discussing global treaties, lawyers working with a variety of clients, and teachers providing quality education to every child in their classrooms. It provides the opportunity for America to realize its highest democratic ideals.

Perhaps most important for you as an individual, if you choose to take advantage of the diverse student body of your campus, you are likely to have a much richer and expansive life. Your opportunity for friendship and broad thinking will have no artificial restrictions or boundaries. You will be intellectually and socially prepared to make a difference in the world around you.

6 Develop Good Study Habits

It may come as a surprise that for many students, college success is as much a result of good study skills as it is of intellectual ability or "smarts." That's right. One of the most important keys to academic success in college is having good study skills. Your college already has made the determination that you are intellectually qualified to do good academic work at your school. But translating your intellectual abilities into passing grades requires a fair amount of expertise in the how-to of studying.

Developing good study skills has much to do with knowing yourself and being honest with yourself. There's no single best answer for everyone regarding study skills, but there certainly is a best approach for you as an individual.

Where and under what conditions do you study best? Some students can concentrate quite well in their residence hall rooms with music playing, interruptions and shouts from neighbors, and a generally chaotic setting. Other students need to leave their living space and head to a library or an empty classroom to find the quiet and solitude necessary to concentrate, study, and write.

When you sit down to study, the first thing to do is get yourself organized. Review your assignments. What is due the next day, the next week, the next month? How long is each assignment likely to take? Which assignment are you mentally and physically prepared to focus on first, so that the most difficult assignment will have your deepest concentration. Know whether your study style is to immerse yourself in a single project for hours at a time or to work in 20- or 30-minute chunks. Pace yourself. Plan breaks.

Don't allow yourself to get discouraged. It takes time to get acclimated to the pace of work and higher expectations in college. It might take a few assignments to get the hang of it, and you might even get a low grade on a first test or paper, a grade that you never saw in high school. Remember, there's always room to learn from these experiences and to adjust your study schedule and approach as the semester goes along. Don't lose hope over one bad grade or one late night of studying.

In math and science, students often have problem sets to complete daily and weekly, and they jump head first into that work. It's certainly essential to keep up with these daily assignments. You definitely want to avoid falling behind and having to race to catch up in those subjects.

There are always some students who believe that while they must keep up with their daily assignments, they can easily put off essays and research papers until a few days or even the night before the due date. Putting off the work of some classes is a certain path to eventual trouble. Writing papers requires a process of thinking, rethinking, drafting, revising, rethinking again, redrafting again, and so on. Every paper you turn in should represent, at the very least, your third draft. And reaching the third draft should represent a process of thinking, composing, and rethinking the content, language, style, and of course the mechanics of the paper, including grammar, spelling, etc.

As you are about to begin on a specific assignment, go back and carefully reread the assignment. It is absolutely frustrating to work for hours on something only to realize that you didn't fully and precisely address the written assignment. Be certain you understand what is expected, and don't hesitate to contact the professor for clarification if you have any questions.

Some students aren't prepared for all the reading that is required in college courses. It is essential that you learn to read the wide range of text assignments in different ways. Reading history or chemistry textbooks requires a different approach than reading nonfiction or fiction books. Scholarly journal articles and academic monographs require yet another level of focus and concentration to fully comprehend the research findings, empirical analysis, and theoretical discussion they reflect.

Don't sell yourself short in the area of study habits. Do a good, honest assessment of your study habits, and make adjustments and improvements as needed. If you find yourself in need of help in this area, don't hesitate to ask for advice and suggestions very early in your college career.

7 Ask for Help

In high school, asking for academic help is often what distinguishes the kids who are in academic difficulty or considered "at risk" from the "smart" kids. Fortunately, with so many students now taking college preparation courses for SAT, AP, ACT, and other standardized tests, some of the stigma attached to tutoring and asking for assistance has diminished among college-bound students.

In college, the whole notion of asking for academic help is entirely different from high school. Being able to ask for help is crucial, and the first step is admitting to yourself that you should want and need help. Higher education is about scholarly inquiry, and universities are comprised of people who are genuinely interested in discovering, studying, learning, analyzing, creating, and sharing new knowledge. It is in that context that everyone in college—faculty and students alike—are in constant search of deeper, clearer understandings and new insights. If you don't understand the complexities of an argument, you are expected to ask. If you miss the meaning of a lecture, then of course you should ask. If the math assignment or readings are not clear, then without question you should ask.

Your first stop for academic assistance, and it should be one you make frequently, should be with an academic advisor. Advisors know the academic rules for course and graduation requirements. But they also have extensive experience talking and guiding students through their college careers. They will try to help you make decisions about your college plans rather than outline plans for you. After all, this is **your college education,** not theirs, not your parents', not your teachers', and not your friends'. It is crucial that you figure out what holds most meaning for your studies, your career, and your life. If, for any reason, your advisor is not a good fit for you, then you should find one who is.

Many colleges today have different learning labs in which students can just drop in at most hours of the day or night or schedule appointments with specialists. In traditional language labs, there may be a variety of computer programs, software, videos, tutors, and so on. In math labs, students can do their math homework online, using computer programs, working in study groups, or utilizing one-to-one tutorial help. Writing centers have been in place for a long time, helping students conceptualize and organize papers, giving feedback to students on drafts of paper assignments, and assisting students on technical skills such as grammar and composition. More recently, science resource centers have been established to help students in all the science disciplines. Students use computer software designed for specific classes to solve problems, complete homework, and study for exams. Science texts are available for student use, study groups meet at the center, and tutors are on hand for personal assistance.

College libraries are much more comprehensive, sophisticated, and technologically advanced than most neighborhood libraries. College librarians see themselves as teachers and educators and are eager to offer personal assistance to students. Librarians help students learn to access computer databases and find sources in print and online for research papers. They also offer more basic assistance, such as giving tours of the library and helping find books. Most college librarians are on the cutting edge of technological advances and can be of great assistance in helping you get your hands and eyes on the many resources available to students and scholars today.

Remember, if you're not asking for help and taking advantage of academic support services, advising, study groups, and tutors, you're not being a smart student. Most of your learning will take place outside of the classroom, and you must be skilled and assertive to make sure that your academic learning outside of the classroom is as high quality and intensive as that inside the classroom.

SARA FISHMAN—*"Help! I Can't Take Another Four Years of High School!"*

Sara Fishman so looked forward to meeting new friends at college. Like most of the students at her new college, she came from a racially and economically homogeneous neighborhood and high school, one that was 60% Jewish and 95% white and upper middle class. She recognized the benefits of meeting people from different backgrounds, and she also was ready to break out of the high school cliques that she had both thrived on and grown very tired of in her senior year.

When Sara arrived for summer orientation, she was excited to meet students from different states and different races. She was placed in a room with Jenny, a Chinese-American student from Washington, DC, who was very sophisticated, friendly, and bright. Sara and her roommate got along just fine, and even though it wasn't clear they would become best friends, both girls looked forward to building on this new friendship in the fall. Sara felt that she had taken a big first step toward breaking out of her high school mold.

When Sara arrived at college in the fall, she continued to have high expectations. During her school's "welcome days," she met many new students in her residence hall and tried to go to a variety of social activities that were new to her. She went to a lot of fraternity and sorority parties, but she also went to a dance sponsored by the Indian American students that drew hundreds of students and opened her eyes and was lots and lots of fun. Pretty soon, however, Sara's friends from high school who were attending the same college began texting and calling for the old group to get together. Sara missed her friends and was happy to hear from them. Before she knew it, she found herself spending more and more time with her high school friends and was less available to spend time with new people she had met on her floor.

By the second week of classes, Sara was besieged by calls and flyers urging her to participate in sorority rush. Sara's mom and sister had rushed sororities, and she and they had always expected that Sara would rush, too.

At this point Sara was feeling somewhat overwhelmed by all the new things she was encountering at college, and she was feeling a little homesick. Sara found it comforting to hang out with friends from high school amid the familiar talk and social scene that she had always been so good at. She got caught up in the excitement of rush and the comfort of her old friends and decided to join the sorority with her Jewish, white, and relatively wealthy high school crowd. She felt great. Everyone was super nice to Sara, and she spent a lot of time at her sorority for parties and other social functions.

Midway through the first semester, Sara ran into Jenny, her roommate from orientation. They hugged and asked how each was doing. They exchanged email addresses, but Sara knew they would not get in touch. Sara walked away, wondering what had happened to all her plans to break out of her high school mold. She was feeling more settled in college and was getting adjusted to classes and the pressure of homework and tests. She knew her way around the residence hall and campus and was no longer homesick.

On the one hand, everything seemed to be going great; on the other hand, Sara realized she had not grown much. Already, she was tiring of her high school friends and all the parties. Hadn't she done all that for four years in high school? She knew all their stories, jokes, cliques, and gossip. They even all seemed to think alike. She thought about Jenny, about the Indian dance she had attended, and about all the other friendly students in her residence hall who came from all over the country and who had had so many different experiences growing up.

Sara plopped down on her bed and let out a big sigh. Sure, she loved her old friends and she loved her Jewish life, but she wanted more from college and from life. It had been all too easy to stay trapped in the same mold and never grow in college. She knew this was not what she wanted. Sara made a commitment to herself that she would not let this happen. Could she have it both ways? She decided to stay with the sorority but to cut back on spending so much of her time there. She decided to join other student organizations. She hung out at night with the kids from her residence hall floor. And she frantically searched for Jenny's email address, sent her a note, and made a date to get together.

COLLEGE KNOWLEDGE FOR THE JEWISH STUDENT

8 Discover the Value of Challenging Ideas (Including Your Own)

On the first day of college classes, you are only three months out of high school. Over the course of a single summer, your teachers, parents, rabbis, and peers will stop looking at you as a school child and start seeing you as an adult. This is the time to begin taking responsibility to think and express your own ideas, your own thoughts, and your own opinions.

For years adults and peers have taught you and persuaded you to think and act in particular ways. You've been taught how to interpret history, what books to read, how to practice and believe as a Jew, and even whom your friends should be. But now it's your turn to be an independent adult thinker. You can assert your own ideas, interpretations, and analyses; read whatever books and authors you like; be more or less religiously observant or involved in the Jewish community; and make friends and acquaintances with whomever you choose. You also can and should get involved in the issues of the world.

This new stage in your life provides you with tremendous freedom but also bestows significant responsibility on you. Just as you can begin to assert your independence of mind and spirit, you also must be prepared to defend your ideas, opinions, values, decisions, and actions. That can be quite difficult, but you should embrace this opportunity. Don't shy away from it.

During this process of independence taking, try out some new ideas. Think hard. Challenge yourself. Don't let yourself off the hook easily. Be your harshest critic. You'll find that college faculty are expert at critiquing others' points of view. They can pick apart the most complicated argument, analyze and debate theoretical abstractions, and see right through baseless verbiage and undefended ideas. Don't find yourself on the weak side of a critique without having tested out an idea in your mind first. At the same time, don't back off from your own ideas just because a professor or friend raises questions for you.

What is so exciting about this process is that you get to explore your own identity and discover the person you really are and will be in your adult life. Why do others think the way they do? Why do some people have such very different political views, social relationships, religious practices, cultural traditions, musical and culinary tastes? Take these years to find the beauty in the way all people see the world. Put yourself in their shoes. Try to understand, as they do, how to make sense of the world—theirs and yours. Learn why they celebrate certain events and policies and challenge, sometimes fiercely, other events and policies.

Then go back into your own shoes and start asking questions. Push others to defend their positions. Push yourself to defend your position. Why do you believe and behave as you do? Is it because others—often people who care deeply for you—have guided you along a certain path? You may be ready now to accept their guidance as your own and continue along that path as a result of your own searching. But you may also decide that you want to set out on a different path or take a different path to what is ultimately the same goal. What's important is that you take responsibility and ownership of your life and your society and that you begin to set forth on a journey that is distinctly yours.

In the classroom as in your life journey, it is also time to ask hard questions. Challenge your professors, Hillel leaders, parents, and peers about what they tell you as fact or what they offer as interpretation. How did they come to that opinion? Look for the evidence and the research behind their analysis. Do the careful reading that is essential to asking good questions. Challenge the authors that you read. Become a critical and serious thinker. Be thoughtful in your self-reflection, and be critical in questioning the ideas, assertions, and analyses that others thrust upon you.

9 Live a Balanced Life

Balance is a core principle for having a successful college experience.

It is crucial to take care of your mind AND body while you're in college. The stress and intensity are very real, and it's important to remember to eat and to eat well, to find time for sleeping, working out, laughing, smiling, and so on. It's good to "get away" from the college environment at least twice a month, even if it's just for an hour or two. Go to the nearest downtown, watch a movie off campus, work on a community service project that takes you off campus, take a long walk, or go home.

Treat yourself with respect. You deserve it. (And, by the way, treat your peers with the very same level of respect.) Don't abuse your body by not eating or sleeping. Be careful about substance abuse. Don't entrust your body to alcohol. Be as smart about your lifestyle as you are about classes if you want to remain competitive in college and in your profession. Avoid drugs. Why do you need any of this? You're a bright, high-achieving person with your whole adult life ahead of you. Don't blow it. Don't allow someone to do violence to you, verbally or physically, and don't allow violence to enter your environment.

Work out. Take walks. Go to the gym to lift weights or shoot hoops, or join an intramural team. Dress appropriately. If it's raining or snowing outside, carry an umbrella and wear a hat and gloves. Eat three meals a day. Complain about dorm food if you must, but there's always plenty to eat and enough variety to find something you like.

If you're feeling sick, go to the college's health service. Really, don't mess around with your health. Rest a lot. Eat chicken soup and other foods that will help heal you. Drink fluids. Smile and laugh a bit. Your body is telling you to slow down and take care of yourself. Listen carefully, because sometimes your body is smarter than your brain.

10   Remember That Tomorrow Will Be Even Better Than Today

The adrenaline rush in the first year of college is perhaps unequaled at any other point in one's life. The highs and lows of classes and the ups and downs of social relationships are as exulting as they can seem devastating. It's about growing up, intense learning and study, independence, self-reflection, and the onset of adulthood. It's about all the new people you are meeting and all the new ideas you are confronting. Some are glorious and provoke highs you haven't ever felt before. And, at the same time, other moments are sad, depressing, and painful. Know that you'll always get past the tough moments.

In the beginning of the semester, there is moving to campus, meeting the new roommate, taking the first exam, writing the first paper, going to the first football game. Some days will be never-ending, seeming to go on forever and ever. And then there will be a broken relationship, a critical comment from a professor, a bad phone call from home, a rejection, or a conflict with the college bureaucracy. How could it get so bad, you will wonder in your tears? And, then, before your tears have dried, there is an invitation in the mail, an A on a quiz, a quiet walk across campus, or admission into a summer internship. All of this, and it's only the second week of college! How could this be?

Take it one day at a time and cherish each moment (except the forgettable ones—learn from those moments and then forget them forever). Keep a diary, take pictures, and store the best experiences in your permanent memory bank. Make a list of your best ideas for tomorrow and for the long term. Tomorrow will be here before you know it. Trust that you'll quickly get past the trying moments. Make the good days last a lifetime, as your smile, laughter, and good ideas make the world a better place for all of us.

2

Who Am I? Discovering Yourself, Your Jewish Identity, and Other Social Identities

11 Decide Who You Are—It's *Your* Life Now

Now it's your turn. For better or worse—actually, it's all for the better—college is a time when you make the transition from teenager to adult, from boy to man, from girl to woman. You begin to make your own rules. You get to decide your own values. Most important, you get to create your own opportunities and take responsibility for your own mistakes.

The knowledge that you are in charge of your life can be both thrilling and frightening. That's how freedom is. That's what the journey of life is about. You can stay up all night, live on a diet that consists of ice cream only, and skip all your classes. But is that the life you want? Well, it's your choice, good or bad. Now, when you break the rules, they are your rules. And when you set forth on your own path, it's your path and choices and your accomplishments and failures, and the meaning and fulfillment are your own.

One interesting manifestation of this change takes place in the clothing choices of college students. When high school students come to campus for their college tours and interviews, they often take on the "look" of what they believe to represent adulthood. Students are smartly dressed, and all wear up-to-date fashions. These 17-year-old high school students look like they are the graduating college seniors or older.

Fast forward one year to the first year as college students. Both men and women are less aware of their appearance and of the latest styles. What's going on? In high school, students are trying to act like they are adults because they know they aren't yet, so they need to make more effort to dress the part. In college, however, students truly are beginning to be adults in thought and action, and thus they needn't dress up to fill the part because they are playing the adult role legitimately. As adults, they have the freedom to dress up or down as the situation dictates without worrying quite so much about putting on pretenses.

Without a doubt, parents, teachers, rabbis, and friends will still all be trying to advise you and influence your decisions and your life's journey. Listen carefully to what they say because they mean well, have a lifetime of experience to share with you, and can serve as important resources and support for you. But, ultimately, this is your time now. Enjoy the experience of growing up, becoming an adult, and being grown up. Every year will be different and exciting. Enjoy and cherish every moment!

12 Discover Your Values— Jewish and Secular

Who am I? What is the meaning of life? What does it mean to me to be Jewish? What is my responsibility to my community and the world around me? What am I doing here at this college?

The weight of important existential questions of life can feel like a heavy burden in the first year of college, but they are essential for moving forward in life. Indeed, it is critical that you start the process of questioning during college.

I often ask my first-year students to write essays about their individual and group identities. My students embrace this assignment because it allows them to look back on their experiences and reflect on their values, their ideals, and their identities. They write outstanding papers for this assignment, and I advise you to do the same. But, invariably, they will ask me how I can possibly grade them on their identity. I tell them that I value each one of my students as an A+ person, an extraordinary individual with a unique and exceptional life story. But I grade the essay, not the person. It is the ability of each student to tell his or her story in the most thoughtful and reflective manner that will determine the grade.

That's what I would say to you, too. During the first year of college, you should begin in earnest to shape and tell the story of what you find when you look deeply inside to discover who you are now and who you want to be in your lifetime. The deeper you allow yourself to probe and explore, the better able you will be to move with a strong foundation into adulthood. Don't be concerned if the answers aren't easily or immediately found. This is a process that should and does take time.

Think back to what you've been taught about Jewish values. Which of these values do you embody in your daily behavior and attitudes?

Is that by choice or by habit? Which values have you set aside, either because you might disagree or just because you haven't thought about them very much? Do you feel confident that you are sufficiently well-educated about Jewish values to make informed choices? Give yourself the opportunity in college to reflect on your values, to learn more about Jewish values, and to choose for yourself what and how you want to incorporate Jewish values into your life.

This process of introspection almost without exception does begin to take place in earnest during the college years, so it's best for you to take control of it.

In college you will find that you have much, much more unstructured free time on your hands than you have ever experienced before. While for some people the opportunity to constantly be busy is very worthwhile, having at least some time on your hands can be very useful in giving you a chance to think about your purpose in life, your values, and your Jewish and other social identities.

13 Determine What You Like (and Dislike) in Life

One of the most exciting opportunities of adulthood is identifying those things that you like and don't like. This has been an ongoing process since you were very young, but you were always making choices in the context of your parents and other adults setting the parameters of your choices and influencing your decisions.

To make choices of your own requires being open to trying "new" things so you have a broad enough experience to make good choices for yourself. It also means stepping back and seeing all the "old" things you've been doing in your life with new eyes and perspectives.

Your likes and dislikes come in many shapes and forms, big and small, significant and less significant. For instance, at college you get to decide what toothpaste to use at the sink and what soap and shampoo to use in the shower. You get to decide what food you want to eat at every meal—all sugar all the time, fried or baked, milk or coffee, tofu or steak, green beans or green Jell-O.

You get to choose how to groom yourself and what clothes to wear each day. Do you want a crew cut, Afro, shaved head, or full, flowing tresses? Do you want to grow a beard or be clean shaven? Will you wear jeans or skirts to class? Will you choose ripped pants or ironed shirts? Will you try wild patterns that call attention or bland colors that don't? Your parents may have strong views about all of these choices, but now you are on your own and they are your decisions.

You get to choose classes you want each semester and then decide on your major. Many people will tell you what you should study, and most colleges will impose requirements that limit your choices. Still, despite what your parents, academic advisors, and friends suggest, it's up to you to make the selections that make most sense to you.

The same holds true for almost every aspect of your life. You decide how hard you want to study for your exams, whether to read the assigned and/or recommended readings, and how much effort you want to put into class papers. You choose whether to play sports and whether to attend intercollegiate football or field hockey games on campus. Do you want to celebrate Shabbat with friends at Hillel or go out to the bar on Friday nights, or possibly both? Will you go to Cancun for spring break or do community service through Alternative Spring Break? You get to choose your friends. You get to decide whether or not to drink alcohol and/or get drunk. You get to decide if you want to use drugs. You choose where and with whom you want to live. Will you raise money for the homeless shelter or spend money for new clothes? Will you choose to run for student government office or decide you never want to read the news? Will you decide to rush a fraternity or choose to stay far away from the Greek houses? Will you stay up all night or go to bed at eleven o'clock?

Ultimately, these questions are about the kind of person you want to be. College offers you a chance to reaffirm the choices you've been making in the first part of your life or to put those aside and try out some new choices. If you do this right, it will be a continual process that lasts throughout your lifetime. Give yourself time and space to do this. Most of all, give yourself the power to shape your own life.

AMANDA LANDERS—*"Taming the Party Animal"*

Amanda Landers comes from a wealthy, sophisticated family. She is popular, pretty, and social. She's known to her friends from home as a silly, fun girl with one mystery—she also gets good grades. When she was admitted to an elite university, her "stretch" school, her friends, counselors, and even her parents were very surprised, to put it mildly. Amanda just laughed off all the jokes but followed along in their social expectations. She spent a lot of time and money on new clothes for college and talked with her friends incessantly about what sorority she would pledge and how much she looked forward to college partying.

After a long summer of waiting for the start of college, the first day of classes arrived, and Amanda was terrified. Faculty handed out syllabi with difficult readings and long papers due almost immediately. Although Amanda publicly kept up her pretense of the silly, social girl at first, she also knew she had to confront her doubts. She knew there was no way that a party girl could succeed at this school. And she had already met so many smart, serious students at orientation that she questioned whether she should just give up—leave college and fly home. But Amanda also knew that she was smart. Her teachers had told her that she was an excellent writer. She knew how to study for exams. She had strong determination to be a successful, professional woman and understood the necessity of doing well in college.

Amanda tried to play it both ways during her first semester. She did act like the silly, party girl on weekends but tried her hardest when she went back to her room to study and be prepared for class. One of her professors noted on a paper, "Amanda, this is an outstanding, analytic paper. I wish you would share more of your good insights in class instead of talking and giggling so much. You have so much to contribute." When the semester came to a close, Amanda decided that it was time for her to find a better balance in her life, to shake the "silly" facade and to start living her life, both inwardly and outwardly, as the more confident, serious person she knew she was.

Amanda saw that she could fairly easily pass her courses with Bs and Cs, but she knew she was much better than that. The next semester she enrolled in more difficult courses and spent more time on her studies and less on parties, though she still had an active social life on weekends. She appreciated that her professors noticed, her parents praised her, and her friends still liked her. Amanda felt good about herself, her future, and how well she was managing the different aspects of her life as an intelligent woman and young adult.

You will find yourself at college with a whole new set of people surrounding you—new friends, new classmates, new teachers, new adults. You have an opportunity to explore, experiment, establish, and assert who you are, what your identity is, and who you want to be in life.

The values you hold, what you intrinsically believe, and how you see and define yourself, regardless of anyone else's viewpoint, should be the most important factors in establishing your identity. The views of outsiders become particularly important when they come from people you know and trust. But even those views should stand apart from your own independent and internal sense of your values and identity.

However, in addition to your special and unique individual identity, you also have various social identities. This means that your individual identity is linked to the social identity of many other people. These social identities range from ethnic identity to racial identity, religious identity, economic class identity, gender identity, sexual orientation identity, and so forth. For many of you, your social identity includes more than one group within each of these categories, such as more than one ethnic or racial identity.

Social identities are very significant in our lives. You may choose not to embrace the values, histories, cultures, traditions, and other beliefs and practices associated with a group that is part of your social identity. However, as you know from Jewish history, people and institutions outside the group will typically hold attitudes and act in certain ways toward you simply on the basis of your social identity, regardless of your degree of commitment to the group. The history of our civilization and of this country tells repeated stories of oppression and injustices toward people based solely on their social identities.

Social identities matter. Even though everyone at your college has in common the fact that they are outstanding students attending the same college and taking similar classes, there will be strong pressures to try to limit the kinds of people with whom you become friends and associate based solely on their social identities. We all have made assumptions and often acted in particular ways toward other individuals based strictly on their race, gender, religion, and economic class.

Some Jewish students are strongly encouraged by their families and home community to associate primarily with other Jewish students because Jews are their people and community and their familiar comfort zone, and because it may increase the chances of meeting a lifelong Jewish partner. I have met many Jewish students who feel torn and pulled between their desire to meet people from all different backgrounds at college and the advice of parents and the personal comfort of staying close just with what is most familiar—other Jews.

I think this is a good situation to invoke the "both/and" principle. You don't have to feel you need to choose either one community or another. Think **both/and** as you embrace both your Jewish identity, your Jewish community, and your Jewish friends **as well as** students and communities from all different racial, religious, class, and other social identity backgrounds. You can definitely have the best of both worlds.

If you are clear and thoughtful about your privileges and social disadvantages that are based on your various social identities, you may have the courage and conviction to cross and challenge some of these barriers. In so doing, you will find that you are able to both explore a much broader set of friendships than you had while growing up and help to establish a world based on social justice for people from all backgrounds.

15 Take Ownership of Your Jewish Identity

You've had your Bar or Bat Mitzvah, attended Hebrew School or Jewish day school, perhaps were active in Jewish youth groups and went to Jewish summer camps, and have even been to Israel. Or maybe you didn't do any of that. You may have embraced every aspect of your Jewish childhood and teenage years, or you may have fought with your parents every Jewish step of the way.

Regardless of your Jewish beliefs and practices at home, college is a time for you to begin the journey of making choices of your own about your Jewish identity. You may choose to reaffirm what you've been taught until now, to challenge your family's ways so as to strengthen or lessen your commitments and practice, or to explore and examine more carefully what exactly your Jewish identity means to you.

The decision about which college to attend can involve an important Jewish identity choice in terms of Jewish demographics on campus, opportunities for Judaic studies courses, the atmosphere surrounding Israel politics, and the religious offerings for students from all Jewish religious denominations. These are important considerations certainly, but the hard work of determining your own personal Jewish identity begins once you arrive on campus.

For many Jewish students, the first college encounter with Jewish life is an invitation to attend a Hillel welcome event at the start of the school year and the first Shabbat. For others, it is a decision to study Hebrew as a second language, to take a Jewish History or Sociology course, or whether or not to join a Jewish fraternity or sorority. For others still, it is the onset of Rosh Hashanah and Yom Kippur and a choice of whether or not to attend services for those who remain on campus and don't go home for the holidays.

What's most important for you to appreciate is that, like many other choices at college, you get to decide how you want to think about your Jewish identity. While it is certainly true that your parents, grandparents, friends, siblings, rabbis, and the organized Jewish community have a very clear opinion about what they want you to do, it's your Jewish life and, ultimately, your choice to decide. Further, to the extent that you do decide to examine and make your own choices about your Jewish identity, your identity will be that much stronger and secure.

One of the great opportunities for Jewish college students is that there is much greater interaction, both religiously and socially, among Jews across religious denominations, between those who attended day school and Sunday Hebrew school and between those with different views about gender roles, sexual orientation, and the State of Israel. You should take advantage of the chance to explore the different religious practices and political approaches and experiences of your peers. See what it's like to be Shomer Shabbas and to keep kosher; to learn what it's like to have women reading from the Torah; what a service with musical instruments feels like in terms of kavanah and meaning; or how Jewish students who feel just as strongly attached to Israel can come to such divergent perspectives on political issues. Make friends with these fellow Jews, as well as Jews from different socioeconomic classes, sexual orientations, or racial, ethnic, and national backgrounds. Discuss your different upbringings and experiences as well as your common bonds as young Jewish adults.

In recent years many younger Jews, in contrast to their parents, have identified Jewishly more through friendships and social networks rather than through traditional measures of Jewish identity such as attendance at religious services, attachment to Israel, or membership in Jewish organizations. Increasingly, many young Jews are creating their own services with alternative traditions, celebrating Shabbat dinners in homes rather than Hillel, forming Havurot, and building their own clubs and organizations. And there are also many students in fraternities and sororities who seem to have made it a Jewish college tradition to light Shabbat candles and then go out to the bars on Friday night to meet other Jews.

Whether to date only other Jews will certainly be an important choice and one of great interest and concern to parents, friends, and others in the Jewish community. Discovering yourself as a Jewish male or Jewish female and confronting the roles, expectations, and stereotypes (think "Jewish American Princess") associated with your gender as a Jew, from both within the Jewish community and outside, is a critical growing step. Consider whether you can take advantage of the opportunities to travel to Israel and other Jewish communities outside the United States.

My experience with Jewish college students is that the greatest numbers continue to feel strongly identified as Jews on an individual basis, even though they are not necessarily involved with Jewish organizations or groups. This includes many Jewish students who were active as Jewish leaders in youth groups and involved in day schools and summer camps. A smaller number find their Jewish place as a social network in Jewish fraternities or sororities or in community service or political groups. Another group finds a real home at Hillel or other Jewish organizations and is very active and involved. Very few, in my experience, make a conscious decision to reject or abandon their Jewish identity.

Your choices about your Jewish identity will likely be a lifelong journey, with periods of more or less intensity, commitment, and meaning. Take this opportunity in college to begin this exploration and to own the good decisions you will make.

16 Manage Conflicts with Jewish Holidays

Everything is going along smoothly during your first days of college. You're beginning to find your way around campus, have made some new friends, and have attended your first classes. Now your parents are calling to ask about your plans for the Jewish holidays.

It's neither the fact that your parents are calling nor the Jewish holidays that are a problem; rather, for many Jewish students, it will be the first time that they will face a serious conflict between their Jewish faith and a non-Jewish society. Many Jewish students come from homogenous communities in which there has been institutional recognition and sensitivity to the conflict Jewish students face, and there are mechanisms in place to address missing classes and assignments. For others, the school calendars are accommodating of Jewish students to the point of canceling classes on the Jewish High Holidays.

At most colleges, however, Jewish students are a numerical minority and the academic calendar marches on without skipping a beat for the Jewish holidays. At the same time, many campuses do make faculty aware of holidays of various religious groups, and ask their faculty to be aware of possible conflicts and to show sensitivity and make accommodations when possible.

The conflict raises a number of issues for Jewish students: (1) whether or not to travel home to be with family during the holidays; (2) whether to skip class to attend services and observe the holidays; (3) how to manage conflicts over class attendance and assignments during the holidays with faculty and/or administrators who are unfamiliar, confused, or insensitive to the observance of Jewish students; and (4) how to fully embrace the spirit of the holidays in an environment that largely seems oblivious to the most important holidays of the Jewish year.

The decision as to whether or not to travel home is often out of your hands. It may be too costly to travel, the timing of the holidays may create a conflict because they vary considerably each year, and the move-in dates and starts of classes vary from campus to campus. Given these external considerations, you will want to consider whether you want to use the holidays as a time to begin building a Jewish home for yourself on campus by meeting other Jewish students and becoming part of the campus Jewish community, or returning to the rich and meaningful Jewish life you know at home with your family and to celebrate the holidays in a deep way there.

Depending on the timing of the holidays and your college's academic calendar, you may have either just started classes or be fast approaching the first set of exams. In either case, you will rightfully be concerned with missing class at these important moments of the start of your college career. At the same time, this is the beginning of the life stage where you will want to stand by your ethical, moral, and religious convictions. If celebrating the High Holy Days (and other holidays) is important to you, then you will figure out how to work around the conflict with classes. Yes, there may be compromises and extra work such as studying more and socializing less in the days leading up to and right after the holidays. And you might have to speak up to your professors (whom you barely know) to explain why you will not be in class those days. However, these are the kinds of choices that Jewish adults make in this society and that you will confront throughout your life.

Most professors are very familiar with requests from Jewish students to miss class during Rosh Hashanah and Yom Kippur and are ready to accommodate you if you give advance notice. Even so, other faculty members are very confused about Jewish law, in part because Jewish students themselves observe the holidays with wide variation. For instance, based on what their Jewish students tell them, professors may not understand that holidays begin at sundown and it may not be clear whether Rosh Hashanah is observed one day or two. (Confusion is even more pronounced during Sukkot and Shmini Atzeret.) They also might not understand why for a fasting, observant student, rescheduling an exam for the day after Yom Kippur is not the generous accommodation they intended. Offering calm and clear explanations will go a long way to resolve confusion. And, in the event you encounter the rare professor who seems to be insensitive or antagonistic despite your best explanations, don't hesitate to talk with your campus Hillel director, the department chair, the dean of the college, or all of the above.

For those Jewish students who seek to fully observe the Days of Awe in the deepest, most meaningful way and are used to doing so in a community that is all Jewish, it will be a challenge at first. It will take additional focus and intentionality not to be distracted by the rhythm of a secular college environment and peers that are moving forward with the press of school-welcoming activities and new classes. New friends in your residence hall will be happy that you have to celebrate your holiday, but they won't understand why you can't also go to the social event that evening or participate in the study group that you so much wanted to be a part of.

Affirm your values, find your focus, take steps to build your new Jewish community, and do what you know is right for you as you best understand your Jewish identity. Whatever you decide will be OK, you will learn from the choices you make, and you will continue to wrestle with these issues and choices as you grow as a full Jewish adult in a pluralistic society. Shana Tovah!

Surround yourself with good people. Choose to be close friends with people you can trust and who will care about your well-being. Look at their values and judgments. Be sure you respect them.

Good friends make all the difference in the world. Of course, you can and will have a great many acquaintances, and it's best not to have only a small inner circle of friends. Be open to interacting with and learning from all different kinds of people. And when you choose your close friends, pick good people. It will hold you in good stead throughout your life.

At the same time, don't be overly picky. In college you will meet hundreds or even thousands of other students. You might find that you don't particularly like some of them. That's okay. But if your school had 2,000 students and you don't like, say, 1,500 of them (though that's pretty hard to imagine), you've shut the door on friendships with three-quarters of the student population. In this case, you may want to try a more open approach to developing friendships.

Part of the trick of finding friends is by being a "friendly" person yourself. All that means is that you need to allow yourself to be liked by others. That doesn't mean you have to be Ms. Popularity or Mr. Smiley Face all the time. But it does mean that you should say *hello* back to people who smile at you, that you should go out with people who invite you to go out with them (at least some of the time), and that you should share a little about yourself and open yourself to the possibility of liking others and having others like you.

The other thing about friends is to remember that relationships take work and time. You probably have a pretty good idea of how much time it takes to do well in a class you're taking. Good friendships demand the same—effort and time. Friends should be there for you when you need them, but you need to be there for them too, even at inconvenient times. Relationships take time to grow; they require hanging out and doing things together and building a wealth of experiences together.

If you surround yourself with good people, they will give you good advice. They will steer you in good directions. They will set high expectations for your behavior and values. They will not get you into dangerous situations or ask you to do things you know to be wrong. You will become a better person for those friendships, as will your friends.

BEN MARTIN—"*Relationships Are More Complicated Than I Thought.*"

For Ben Martin and his two lifelong buddies, it seemed that the biggest concern of their parents as they were going off to college was that they should exclusively date other Jews.

There were many reasons for their concern but the primary ones were their fear for the very survival of the Jewish people through interfaith marriage and for Ben's and his friends' personal happiness. How many times had Ben been in synagogue with his parents when the rabbi had given a sermon about the various National Jewish Population Studies that showed that approximately 50% of Jews were marrying non-Jews and how there would be a drastic and dangerous decline in the Jewish population within a matter of several generations unless things turned around.

Ben and his friends talked about this subject a lot in high school but even more so in college. While Ben also thought it would be a good idea for him to marry a Jewish woman, because of his personal history with his parents' unhappy divorce and what he witnessed from friends with single-parent households, his first priority was to find someone that he loved and with whom he was compatible.

For his friend, Michael, the issue was clear; his future wife would either have to be Jewish or be agreeable to converting to Judaism and raising a Jewish family with him. For Andrew, the issue was a little different. He was definitely committed to restricting his dating and marriage to a Jew, but Andrew was gay and so he found himself sometimes dealing with an entirely different set of challenges.

In his first month at college, Ben hung out with lots of Jewish friends, men and women alike. There were a couple of women whom he had some interest in, but nothing really clicked. He started to go out with a Jewish woman, Miriam, who came from a modern Orthodox background. They had a lot of fun together, and they saw each other a lot at Hillel. Ben had never been in a relationship with an orthodox woman and, while all his Jewish friends and family were happy he was dating a Jewish woman, he was surprised to hear the reactions of some of his friends about her being "too religious" for him. His mother was supportive but his father was the first to chime in with religious jokes about the orthodox and Ben was appalled. "She's Jewish, after all," Ben thought, "so what are these jokes all about?" But Miriam also reported that she was getting the same kind of response from some of her friends and family that he wasn't "Jewish enough." Ben and Miriam liked each other a lot, but this was never meant to be a long-lasting relationship; it was as much a good friendship as it ever was a serious relationship. In fact, they probably stayed together longer as a couple than they would have just out of reaction to the comments they had gotten.

Ben's friend, Michael, dated a lot but seemed to be struggling about how to maintain a relationship. He was pretty successful in getting a first date, but neither he nor the women he dated seemed very interested in pursuing the relationship beyond the first date or two. Michael had, in fact, only been dating Jewish women, but for the time being he was much more concerned about the issue of relationships than the religious background of his dates. That wasn't a question for him. Marriage was the last thing on his mind. At this point, he was beginning to worry whether he would ever have a meaningful relationship. He just wished there was an adult he could talk to about dating and relationships. As committed to his Jewish identity as he was, he couldn't think of anyone in his synagogue or Jewish school who had ever talked about relationships beyond the business of marrying another Jew. Ben was the only person he could talk openly with about these issues. Ben was very helpful, and he also suggested that Michael go to the campus counseling center to talk to someone there.

Andrew had been both surprised and thrilled to find a small but supportive Jewish LGBT group on campus. Although there weren't a great many gay Jewish students who were out on campus, Andrew was committed to only dating Jews. Still, when he had gone home for Rosh Hashanah in the fall, he could just barely tolerate the stares and whispers he sensed when he went to schul with his family. His parents and siblings loved and supported him and stood by him, but he knew it would be a while before he went back home for services.

Ben, Michael, and Andrew stayed close throughout their first year of college. They focused on their academics, remained involved in Jewish activities on campus, and had a great first year. Relationships, they found, were much more complicated than their academics. They struggled to find the right answer for themselves as Jews about interfaith dating, but they were mostly concerned with the immediacy of the upcoming weekend's social situation and the complexity of building and sustaining relationships. The thought of marriage seemed like light years away. They felt very fortunate to have each other as good friends and as a support group to figure out all these important issues about relationships.

18 Explore Religion, Spirituality, and a Life of Meaning

In a society so focused on wealth and material goods, many students today are looking for something more meaningful in their lives. Some are looking for the comfort, faith, and solace of God or Judaism to help them make sense of the world, while others are searching for answers in spirituality or a spiritual community.

You may identify closely with Judaism when you arrive at college, or you may be less closely affiliated with the Jewish community and Judaism but still want to find deeper meaning and commitments in your life. This interest in organized religion or a search for spirituality is increasingly true of students who are attending college today.

There are Hillels and other Jewish-affiliated organizations on most campuses. These organizations seek to provide a campus home for you as a Jew. They are student centered, and they usually offer both religious and social activities to encourage your continued involvement in and pursuit of Jewish life, community, and religion while in college with a group of Jewish peers.

Some students either object to organized religion or have found that for them Judaism has not provided the spiritual foundation and grounding they are seeking. Many Jewish students, even though they don't associate closely with Hillel, still stay strongly connected to Judaism and Jewish religious observance through alternative religious services, interdenominational study groups, or Shabbat dinners with small groups of friends. Other Jewish students feel closely connected to Judaism through their social justice and community service activities. Still others may discover what they are looking for, transcending the formalities of religious practice and organized religions, in books, nature, friendships, and meaningful connections with like-minded people who are searching for something deeper in life.

Some students will try to convert you to join a different religion or persuade you to follow a particular religious or spiritual path they have chosen for themselves. I don't know of any Jewish student who has appreciated being proselytized on college campuses by his or her fellow students.

Over the years, some groups have periodically misrepresented their mission and preyed on college students, attempting to recruit impressionable college students to join cults. I still remember being approached by followers of such a group, on my first day on campus prior to attending graduate school classes at the University of California at Berkeley. A couple of welcoming young people, without any mention of their religious group, asked me to come join them at their house for what they described as "a festive dinner with a group of friendly students," an opportunity to meet people in my new town. As a graduate student, I knew what their dangerous ploy was all about, but it was certainly slick and deceptive, and a first-year college student would have been hard-pressed to turn them down. Be forewarned about groups that misrepresent their intentions.

Your search for faith, religion, spirituality, and meaning in life are likely to be of great importance to you, just as they have been to generations of Jews seeking to understand the mysteries and the commonplace of our lives. Use the many resources available at Hillel and other campus groups and organizations. Stay connected to Jewish social networks, blogs, and national/global discussions online. Consult with many peers and elders, but don't just follow what other folks, both the well meaning and the untrustworthy, tell you to do or believe. Find your own answers and path. Be smart and thoughtful about this process, and take your time on this important journey to deepen your life's understanding, purpose, and meaning.

The high school routine is all about being busy—superbusy. Take difficult classes. Join extracurricular activities. Get a job. Do volunteer work. Help around the house. Spend time with friends—when you have a free minute. Everyone is rewarded for being an active, busy person. It helps on your college applications, it brings praise from teachers and parents, and it makes you feel good because you believe you're doing the "right" thing by being so busy.

But what's missing in that picture? The missing ingredient is *you,* and the time to be alone with the very wonderful person you have become. If you really believe the tips in this book, then you'll believe that you're a pretty extraordinary person! So, if you had the opportunity to be with someone as special as you are, wouldn't you jump at that chance in a second?!

There is great value to being alone with yourself. It gives you a moment to pause and reflect. It gives you time to wind down, to relax, to reevaluate, to think, and to contemplate the world. It allows you to do nothing.

What can you do when you are alone with yourself? You can listen to music or even make music. You can be quiet. You can go for a walk. You can lie in your bed and close your eyes—or lie there and stare up at the ceiling. You can pray. You can reimagine your actions and yourself in more positive ways. You can review the past day, your relationships, your classes, your conversations. You can watch TV. You can go to a movie. You can go to an event on campus by yourself. You can eat a meal by yourself. You can do nothing.

Sometimes the act of doing nothing allows you to do the most. It can free the clutter from your mind so that you can think clearly. Sometimes silence is necessary to allow you to hear yourself think. Sometimes closing your eyes allows you to see more clearly than ever before. Sometimes being alone will help you be an even better friend to those you care about and like to be around.

The one requirement to being alone is that you must like yourself. And if you don't like yourself, then the discomfort you feel when you are alone is a wake-up call to get in touch with yourself so you can begin to become a person you can like a whole lot more. People don't want to spend much time with people they don't like. That holds true even for ourselves. Find that special individual inside you, and you will discover one of your very best lifelong friends.

20 Fall in Love

This isn't Hollywood we're talking about. This is your life. Love is one of life's wonderful blessings, and you may very well experience it during your college years.

One thing Hollywood often neglects to tell us is that love is tied to relationships, and relationships are difficult arrangements that require a great deal of attention. You must be prepared to cherish and nurture your loving relationships.

When your favorite romantic movie ends after two hours, it feels as if the story will go on forever. But after the first two hours of your loving relationship, guess what? You don't get to leave the movie theater and live happily ever after in fantasyland. There you and your partner are in full living color, ready or not, with all the challenges and thrills that loving relationships bring us. That's both the good news and the bad news.

With falling in love in college, the reality is that it oftentimes comes with disappointment. Just as love takes you to the farthest reaches of joy and happiness, breaking up with someone you truly love can be deeply sad and painful. And college love and relationships, because they take place at a relatively young age and in unique settings, are usually not the kind that last forever, even though they may be intensely felt and deeply joyous and fulfilling. The good news is that you will almost certainly find other loving relationships; the bad news is that the time of breaking up can hurt and can be distressing and distracting.

When you fall in love in college, it's important to remember that you're still in college. Oh yeah—college. Did you forget already? Enjoy your love, but still find time to do your homework, study for tests, and write research papers. Your heart may be floating, but keep your mind grounded in the real world. Life goes on, as do your classes and your professors' assignments.

Love and relationships require taking risks. They are most certainly worth the risk that the love won't be requited or that the relationship won't be lasting. You would never want to miss out on the joy of a deeply felt loving relationship. Just keep in mind the opportunity this provides to learn how to incorporate love and relationships into your daily life and other responsibilities, commitments, and cares. Remember throughout that you're still a college student!

3

Milk and Honey:
Getting the Most Out of College

21 Make Yourself a Part of the Scholarly Community

College connotes different things to different people. I hope you'll be one of those students who thinks of college as a community—or, more specifically, a scholarly community—in which you get to spend four years of your life with a group of people who are deeply engaged with ideas, exploration, questioning, discovery, analysis, and problem solving. To do so will most definitely put you in the right mind-set for a successful college experience.

Consider for a moment some other ideas about college. For some Jewish students, college is like an extended summer camp or Hollywood movie where the primary goal is to make great friends, party, and have as much fun as possible while you pick up a degree along the way. For others, it is a professional training ground where you are preparing for a lucrative career. Still others think of it as a place of competition and endless judgment, with tests and exams and grades.

Why do I encourage you to approach your college experience as a scholarly community? Let's take the community aspect first. It's important to surround yourself with good people. As you grow and develop personally, socially, and intellectually, it's so much healthier to do so in a supportive environment of thinking, caring people. It is in this sense of community that college is far more than a set of requirements or courses or credits to complete. You have the unique opportunity to think, study, and grow surrounded by and engaged with other bright, thinking people.

In terms of the scholarly aspect of college, it's important that you begin to self-identify as a young scholar or a scholar apprentice. This piece of advice is not intended to pigeonhole you or limit you socially—in fact, it will probably do just the opposite. It will prevent you from becoming overly parochial by allowing you to grow and expand exponentially.

Personal and social growth is, of course, essential, but what makes college unique is the attention to analytic thinking, books, lectures, discussions, critical insights, discoveries, and information. You have the opportunity to be a part of and contribute to a collection of people, faculty, and students who are focused on learning, exploring, and thinking deeply about all sorts of issues, topics, and inquiries.

Once you've received your letter of admission to college, it's actually very easy to become a part of the scholarly community. The hardest part is to make a shift in your mind-set. Instead of thinking of course work as a series of assignments, tests, and homework, you need to think of it as a great opportunity for learning. Instead of thinking of your teachers as people who judge you and have control of grading, imagine them as mentors, fellow thinkers, senior colleagues, and scholarly friends and allies. Check your social network sites or the school newspaper and attend the daily guest lectures and talks on campus. Go to theater productions, art exhibits, and classical concerts. Read national and global newspapers and blogs. Peruse scientific and popular magazines that address intellectual issues. Visit faculty in their offices. Go to receptions, book signings, and poetry readings. Hang out with your friends in your residence hall late at night, and talk about an exciting or controversial idea from a class that day.

22 Think Critically

So you know what it means to think, and you've been doing a lot of hard work throughout high school that required you to think. So why would this be one of this book's tips, and why would you need to be concerned about thinking critically in college?

Consider what sets apart those who are college educated from those who are not. It is the expectation that a college-educated person will think insightfully and analytically about issues and can get to the root of the complex questions and challenges that face us personally and as a society.

Thinking critically is one of the most essential lessons of college. And, unfortunately, in high school, too few students are asked to think critically—even those who score very well on standardized tests, write well-organized essays on exams, and quickly complete advanced math assignments.

Critical thinking means that you are able to consider and analyze ideas, readings, debates, and discoveries in a comprehensive and thorough manner. It means that you can understand the nuances of an author's ideas and then cogently challenge those ideas. It means that you can understand a point of view and then critique that point of view from multiple perspectives. It means you can hold several compelling but competing ideas and arguments in your mind at the same time and then examine the strengths and weaknesses of each. It means that you're usually impatient with two-sided debates because you realize that most issues have more than two sides and that most issues are far more complex than the discussion that any debate format will elicit. It means that you ask difficult questions of yourselves, others, and the physical world around you and that when you find reasonable answers to your questions, you will ask a second and third set of questions that probe more broadly and more deeply.

Some of my *supposedly* best-prepared students (those who come from well-heeled suburban and private high schools) initially turn in college papers that are clear and well organized but that don't typically have much substance. The papers just don't say very much. In high school they were praised and rewarded for such papers, but in college they will be expected to do much more. These papers have good form but insufficient substance and analysis. My sense has been that these students have not ever been challenged to think critically.

By contrast, I have other students whose high schools are not so highly ranked and whose paper writing skills are sometimes lacking, but who have been forced to ask difficult questions and to analyze and challenge normative assumptions in deeper ways.

Both sets of students (of course, these groupings are overly broad generalizations) will have considerable work to do in college. The good news is that they all have the ability to think critically. The problem is that until college, few have been asked to do so.

The best approach to thinking critically is to ask questions to peel back layers of understandings. You should ask these questions about your own ideas, assumptions, and life, and you should also ask them about the ideas of others you meet through novels, articles, textbooks, and lectures. Go back again and again to probe and analyze. Accept your professors' feedback and perhaps initial lower grades with open arms because what they are doing is challenging you to raise your self-expectations for your work.

If you had already finished your learning and intellectual development, you wouldn't need to be in college. Learning to think critically will permit you to lead and excel in so many personal, intellectual, civic, and professional fields. It's one of the greatest gifts of a good college education.

23 Ask Questions

Ever since first grade, teachers have been telling you that there is no such thing as a bad question. And yet you know in your heart that they probably never meant it. For as soon as those words would come out of your teacher's mouth, some innocent, believing student in class would raise his hand and then get ridiculed for asking just that—a "bad" question.

I can't promise you that you won't be ridiculed by faculty, family, and friends for asking questions, but I can tell you that if you don't ask questions, and lots of them, you might as well not be in college.

Questioning is at the core of intellectual life. (And it's central to Jewish life, too. I am certain that you know by heart the Four Questions of the Passover Seder.) It comes from basic human curiosity. Its source is our need to explore what isn't yet understood, discover the unknown, examine the truths behind the truth, and develop the capacity to see from multiple perspectives. Questioning allows our social and scientific worlds to advance from one generation to the next.

Asking questions is also a very practical matter. You need to know where your class is going to be held so you can be there on time on the first day of class. You need to know whether classes start on the hour, on the half hour, or at ten minutes past the hour. You want to know how to address a professor, by title or by first name? You need to know when your first exam is due, and what your professor thinks about using websites as sources for research papers. You most certainly will need to ask how to access the rich virtual and print resources of your library.

Similarly, in your personal life, some of you will need to learn how to do your laundry. Some students will need to learn about opening a bank account and balancing a checkbook or personal budget. You will need to learn where the public bathrooms are throughout the campus. You will need to know what to do when you're standing in the hall in your bathrobe after taking a shower and you realize that you've locked yourself out of your room.

Questioning is also political. Asking the question is a statement that you have the right and the responsibility to question authorities and to question authority. You have the right to ask the department chair why your professor does not hold office hours or frequently misses classes. You have the responsibility to ask the president of your college why the faculty does not include more tenured women. You have the right to challenge the news media's depiction of current events. You have the responsibility to ask students at your lunch table in the residence hall cafeteria why they are laughing at racist or "Jewish American Princess" jokes. You have the responsibility to ask why more students are not voting in campus elections for student leaders or in national presidential and congressional elections.

It's true that some questions will irritate, agitate, and complicate your life and others' lives. But that doesn't mean that the questions are "bad" ones. Just keep asking your questions—that's the role of the scholar.

JASON CASTRO—*"Is That Really True?"*

Jason Castro came to college in awe of his professors. After all, hadn't all the college admissions literature talked about how smart, articulate, and renowned they were? He had held his high school teachers in high regard, and while some of them were truly excellent, he felt that some just didn't know what they were talking about. His college professors had Ph.D.s and wrote books—that sure seemed to be credential enough to Jason.

Jason also believed what he read in textbooks. Weren't you supposed to? He couldn't even imagine that textbooks could have a particular perspective or hold a certain point of view—or even be misleading by only telling some of the facts. It all seemed pretty straightforward to Jason—you go to college to study with brilliant professors and learn all about your major from informative texts.

Jason's first weeks of college went just as he had expected. The professor handed out a clear and challenging syllabus, readings were assigned, and homework and tests were scheduled throughout the semester. Jason went to the college bookstore to buy the assigned books for all his classes. Some students complained about the course load and the amount of studying they had to do, but Jason came to college expecting to do a lot of studying and wasn't worried about it.

In science class one day, the professor had students turn to page 40 of the textbook and asked what they thought of the information and explanation presented. The students were mostly quiet, except for those few who always raised their hands. But the professor wasn't satisfied with their comments—she said that there was an alternative explanation that challenged what the text was presenting as fact. Jason was surprised that the textbook wouldn't be up to date, but he thought that this just showed how brilliant his professor was. Students discussed the alternative explanation and offered a variety of comments to demonstrate why it now seemed preferable to the textbook information.

Then the professor said that she didn't accept the alternative explanation either. And, she went on, she didn't have a good explanation in place of either of those that had been presented thus far, but stated that this confusion was exactly what made science interesting to her! Jason and his classmates were confused. Of all his classes, science had been the most clear, definitive, and unquestioned.

In sociology, Jason thought he did perfectly on his first paper. He had carefully read the texts for class and taken copious notes. But the professor in that class wrote all over the paper, asking why Jason believed what he had written. The professor wanted to know why Jason just accepted different authors' opinions as fact. Hadn't Jason heard the professor challenge the authors' theories and perspectives? The professor wanted Jason's opinion, and he wanted Jason to make strong arguments to support his point of view.

This was all new to Jason. He was skilled at taking notes, reading carefully, and writing up in papers and tests what he thought professors wanted to hear. In his high school, which was first rate, Jason had been rewarded for this skill, and he was a straight-A student. Now he was no longer the straight-A student, and his professors were requiring him to think critically and independently. This was new and difficult for Jason, but he quickly came to see that this was what his professors loved to do for themselves.

Jason began to see that to do well in college, he needed to learn to challenge the information and ideas, arguments, and opinions that were all around him, including his own. This was hard, at least at first, but Jason slowly developed a keen analytic ability. He did this by reading more carefully, actively participating in class discussions, and by not being satisfied with his initial responses and arguments.

Jason became skilled at doing this with his readings and textbooks, but he found it much more difficult to critique his professors. Wasn't that being disrespectful? And wouldn't his professors penalize him if he questioned them? What Jason quickly learned was that professors are human, just like students. Most of them recognized and rewarded Jason for his analytic skills and encouraged him to challenge their ideas. But there were also those who drew the line of critical thinking at the texts. And Jason learned, too, that there was a respectful manner in which he could challenge an idea but not the person expressing it. He liked that.

24 Find Yourself a Mentor

We all benefit from good mentoring. You may have had the good fortune of finding a mentor as a teenager, but more than likely finding a mentor in college will be the first occasion for you to have this special relationship. You should give considerable thought to the idea of mentoring, because you will do well to have mentors throughout your life.

Mentors are people who take an interest in you, as a coach, advisor, and supporter for your professional (and sometimes, personal) well-being. The best mentoring relationships come about through a special relationship that develops between the mentor and mentee. Mentors on occasion may have a personal stake in your professional success, but they most often are simply looking out for your best interests, without any self-interest involved. Mentors differ from parents, advisors, friends, teachers, and counselors, although each of those categories of people may at moments overlap and play roles similar to those of mentors. Mentors fall into a unique category all their own.

When a mentor gives you advice, he or she will first and foremost know what your interests and strengths are and will always tailor the discussion very specifically to your individual needs, guiding you away from problem teachers and giving you tips on how to get into the most popular classes even when they are filled.

Mentors can give you the key to open locked doors. They will let you know when there is a great opportunity for an internship or when special speakers are coming to campus. They will strategize with you when you face obstacles. They will listen to you when you are confused and thwarted. They will give you words of uplift and strength when you are feeling down, and they will help you figure out how to chart your course when you are ready to blaze new paths. Mentors truly care about the well-being and success of their mentees.

Formal mentor programs are a good start for learning about the mentoring relationship. They offer you well-meaning people who will take on the characteristics of a mentor in a formalistic role. At the same time, however, an assigned, formal mentor will rarely support and coach you with the passion and commitment of a mutually developed mentor relationship.

You have to take the initiative and responsibility to look for a mentor. The first step is to know that having a mentor is a good idea. The second step is to realize that a good mentoring relationship, like all good relationships, takes time to develop and requires continuing nurturance. Be patient and do not be demanding.

What you can do is try to develop relationships with people you respect and connect with at college. It's often as easy as following up on a professor's comment of interest or praise about a paper you've written or a comment you've made in class. It can mean something as simple as visiting a professor's office hours to talk without having a very specific question or problem to present. Or, it could mean going to a professor or staff person on campus when you do indeed have a problem and taking a risk to trust someone with your personal story.

Good mentors will want time to get to know you, to determine whether they respect you as a person and as a professional. They will want to see the special spark of inner integrity and values that they admire. They will expect that you will be willing to share something about yourself. They will want to know that this will be a relationship that will continue over time. Mentoring relationships are ones of mutual respect and admiration. They involve generosity and giving.

25   Pursue Your Intellectual Passions

Do you love to read historical novels? Could you spend hours conceptualizing and then tinkering with the mechanics of a science project? Do you write poetry or do graphic arts in your free time? Are you consumed with the environmental crisis that global warming represents? Do you love to look at rock formations? Are you looking forward to the opportunity to study about Jewish life and literature in a serious and substantive way that wasn't available to you in high school? Are you fascinated by the intersection of economics, international conflict, and ethnic hatred?

Dig deep into your life history to come up with a list of subjects that you've found fascinating, troubling, exciting, and just plain worth your time to think about. Begin to identify what you really care about, and then find a way to pursue or at least explore these subject areas in college.

Many students, even those who are liberal arts students, imagine that there are significant constraints on their course selections. First, they are under the impression that they must immediately complete all of their distribution or general education requirements. Second, they feel considerable pressure to take a prescribed set of courses that they believe are required to advance them toward particular majors and preprofessional degrees. Students interested in business, for instance, feel pressured to major in economics. Students interested in law feel pressured to major in political science.

In truth, most students actually have a much greater degree of flexibility for course electives than they imagine when they first enter college. Yes, you do need to pay attention to general education or distribution requirements at your college, and you should draft a plan of how you anticipate fulfilling all or many of those requirements during the first two years. But you have room for electives! Professional programs are much more open to applicants with a broad set of interests than most students imagine. Many law schools would love to have a few more philosophy majors.

Think of your personal list of favorite subjects—your passions and interests—as another set of requirements that you fulfill during college, with equal standing to all the other requirements. You must effectively advocate for your personal set of requirements—your passions and interests—and negotiate the other general education, major, and preprofessional requirements to create a balance in your course schedule and in your life. Be a strong advocate for your own set of favored requirements because this negotiation will be one of the decisive factors in determining whether you feel satisfied with your college education.

Remember, this is **your** college education, and you only get one chance at it! You need to be true to yourself. This is the time in your life to explore those topics that excite you and to pursue those dreams that drive your intellectual passions.

26 Sign Up and Get Involved in a Residential and Curricular Learning Community

Learning communities, perhaps more than any other college offering, emphasize the academic/scholarly community that can exist between faculty and students as part of the college experience. They provide an environment in which you will easily develop friendships with other students. Faculty and staff will get to know you, respect your unique character and potential, and care about you as an individual. And research shows that students participating in learning communities have a significantly higher level of academic success.

How do you make yourself known to others on campus? In your first weeks and months on campus, how do you set yourself apart so that people in your new environment will have a chance to meet the very special and unique person that is you?

Learning communities are innovative and updated versions coming out of both the older and more traditional Oxford model and the alternative, democratic-based experimental colleges of both the Alexander Meiklejohn era and the 1960s. At a time in which public universities can increasingly feel large and corporate-like, these programs hold onto the authentic and very best of college learning. Learning communities give you a chance to meet and study with other students, faculty, and staff on a more personal basis. These programs enable you to get the personal and individualized attention that you deserve as a very bright, new college student. They can make learning come alive!

Residential learning communities, known as living-learning programs, are academic programs located in a residence hall. Students in the program live together in the same hall and take course with faculty who share a common interest in a particular academic theme. Faculty who participate are especially interested in teaching undergraduates, are more accessible, and frequently offer cocurricular programs or outings with students. Students are able to build a tight-knit community of lasting friendships that are built on engagement with new ideas and interaction and dialogue with their peers from different social backgrounds.

Curricular learning communities assign the same set of students to two or more classes or link faculty from different fields to team teach a single group of students in a way that creates intellectual connections between the different subjects. The integrative learning that occurs has proven to be a critical foundation for academic success. In addition, the opportunity to be in two or three classes with the same set of students allows for the development of the strong social connections that are so important to student success.

Some students worry that they don't want to be limited by enrolling in a learning community or may even be looking for a degree of anonymity when they attend college. In my experience, it's very rare that colleges set up programs that impose limits. These programs actually open doors to give you easy access to all the rich resources of the wider campus. These programs seek to get you more deeply engaged in campus activities than you would be if you did not participate in them. As for anonymity, you will have more than enough chances at college to blend in with the crowd and not feel constrained by a very small, closed community. And that is the case even in these programs.

You should definitely look into learning communities. They will help ensure that you continue to be recognized in college for your unique talents as a student and as an individual. They will also enable you to take advantage of the very best educational experiences that colleges have to offer.

Imagine this experience in college: white students in a small class talking with students of color; gay students in conversation with straight students; men and women talking honestly together; Jewish students meeting with their peers from different religious backgrounds; U.S. students engaged in activities with international students. You could be participating in these intergroup dialogues.

Across the country, more and more universities are establishing programs to help students engage in in-depth, serious conversations with fellow students from different social backgrounds.

It's hard for many students like you to find a safe space to ask one another the really hard questions about race, gender, sexual orientation, religious difference, and so on. If you're like the great majority of entering college students, it's highly unlikely that you've had the experience of a deep and sustained conversation with others about the important and enduring issues of difference, commonalities, equalities, and inequalities based on our social identities.

Most students, like you, are very eager for these conversations, yet we all know how hard it is to speak openly about our society's longstanding divisions and conflicts. Intergroup dialogues on college campuses—organized through courses, workshops, or retreats—are structured to give you and other students a chance to meet one another as individuals and as members of various social identity groups, develop a degree of trust in the dialogue group, and build a safe space in which to engage the truly difficult issues that so often divide us.

Students talk about intergroup dialogues as being transformative experiences. What is so exciting about them is that they give you a chance to open the doors to the potential of a diverse society and the dream of American democracy. It's a chance to participate in grassroots democracy, an updated version of the 19th-century New England town hall meeting, where citizens took active control and responsibility for the life of the community and the democratic society. Instead of being held back by the fear and invisible walls that keep people apart, students who participate in dialogues are able to personally engage with their peers on campus and embrace a world that brings all people together.

Another advantage of intergroup dialogue is that, as research findings demonstrate, if you as a student engage with people from different backgrounds, you will learn and understand in deeper and more complex ways than your peers who remain safely in their own comfort zones. Finally, you are more likely to find that the professional world that awaits you as a graduating senior will be looking for someone just like you, a person who can work effectively with people from all different backgrounds as employees, coworkers, and supervisors.

Don't miss this opportunity—it's a chance for you to gain the full benefit of an undergraduate education and to become an active participant and leader in our democratic society.

ILANA STEIN—*"I'm an Engaged Learner because I'm an Engaged Citizen."*

Ilana Stein had devoted herself to her community before coming to college. Through programs at her BBYO Chapter and through the National Honor Society at high school, she spent many hours each week tutoring children, caring for the elderly, and volunteering at the hospital's cancer ward.

Ilana's professional dream was to become a doctor, and she was determined to stay on that path during college. Ilana met with a premed academic advisor during orientation and enrolled in chemistry and calculus for the premed path in addition to her other liberal arts distribution requirements.

When the semester started, Ilana decided not to pursue extracurricular activities because she knew she would need all the time she had for studying. Even though she had already completed calculus and chemistry in high school, she didn't feel confident enough to jump to the second level of college courses in these disciplines. As a result, the first few weeks of school were mostly review and not too difficult for her. Still, Ilana studied hard each night, completed all her homework problems and received an A on her first exam.

As the semester progressed, the workload seemed to grow heavier and heavier, and the level of difficulty also increased. Ilana was pleased that she hadn't gotten involved in extracurricular activities this first term. She saw that she was right that she needed all her time for studying.

Ilana's friends and the girls on her hall often stopped by to ask her to join them to go to concerts or movies, but Ilana always declined. As time went on, however, what surprised Ilana was that it seemed the more time she spent studying, the less she was able to remember, and her homework quality was suffering as well.

Ilana was disappointed and distressed to find that her grades were beginning to slip. She stayed up later and later each night to study, but it didn't seem to help. She met with her teachers, but that didn't seem to make a difference either. She began to wonder whether she was competitive with other students in the premed track.

Ilana's friends couldn't help but notice how stressed she was. Her high school friends commented that she wasn't fun to be with anymore. Her new friends at college—well, she didn't really have many new friends because she had been so busy studying that she hadn't met many people.

One day, Ilana's resident advisor (RA) knocked on her door and invited her to join some others who were going to the hospital to visit and hold sick infants. Ilana liked her RA and didn't want to say no to her. She went along, reluctantly but felt very guilty that she was not studying.

At the hospital, Ilana seemed like an entirely different person. As soon as the group arrived in the newborn ward, Ilana's mood changed. She relaxed, smiled, and was much more sociable with the students she'd gone with. Given all of her experience from high school, she was, of course, very comfortable with the infants and the hospital setting, much more so than many of her peers. Mostly, though, Ilana was distracted from her chemistry and math homework, and it made her seem like a new person.

On the way back to the residence hall, some of the other students were talking about their classes, and it turned out a couple were in Ilana's chemistry class. They were complaining vociferously about the teacher and the low grades everyone had been receiving. Ilana hadn't even been aware that there was a controversy about the teacher or that she wasn't the only one whose grades were falling.

The students just happened to mention they were in a study group, and when they heard Ilana was studying by herself, they invited her to join their group. "Please come, Ilana. It's not a big deal," one said. "It's a pretty loose group, but it sure helps me understand the work better when we work out the homework problems together."

When Ilana sat down that night to finish her homework, she thought a lot about her day. She realized how much she had missed doing community service. Giving back to the community was how she had always defined herself. It had felt so good to hold those babies, and she remembered how much she wanted to make a difference to her community as a doctor.

Ilana also recognized how much she had missed being a social person. It was downright fun hanging out with the other students, and it had been far too long since she had had some fun at college. She also saw clearly that there was real benefit to be had by studying and commiserating with others. She had been feeling isolated, stressed, and discouraged, keeping everything to herself, and it was wonderful to share her experiences with other students and to hear from them that they were feeling much the same.

Chemistry and math certainly didn't get any easier that semester, but her grades began to improve. With her new friends, Ilana was much more mentally and emotionally prepared to cope. Ilana continued to go to the hospital to hold the newborns and became a regular in the study group. She found herself studying just as much as before, but she was more involved civically and socially. She was a much happier and more fulfilled person, and her study time was much more productive. Best of all, she quickly regained confidence in herself and in the fact that she was on the right track, and that medicine was the perfect field of study for her.

28 Take Small Classes and Seminars

The seminar class is the epitome of the college experience. It is what college is all about. There you are, with ten to twenty other intellectually curious students, exploring new ideas and perspectives with a college professor. You raise questions, voice opinions, present critical insights, and listen to the ideas and analyses of your peers and your professor. People in the room challenge each other to think more critically and explore the topic in greater depth.

Your professor guides you beyond surface understandings and interpretations to new and more complex understandings of the day's topic. You realize that your intellectual capacity is so much greater than you ever imagined. You are intellectually invigorated, and you and your classmates carry the class discussion into your thoughts and conversations throughout the day, continuing the conversation as you walk across campus after class.

In a small class you participate as an active learner. Your voice counts and will be heard. You will have the chance to present ideas, discuss readings, and engage with your teacher and fellow students in lively discourse. You will learn how to engage with others who hold different viewpoints. You will learn the important difference between the competitive debate model of discussion and the more collaborative form, intellectual inquiry.

The success of a small class depends as much on the quality of student participation as on the professor's teaching qualities. Unlike most classes you've probably taken before, you carry a significant share of responsibility for class dynamics, the vibrancy of discussion, and the level of analytical thinking that takes place. When you do your work and come prepared to class, your peers and teacher all learn more deeply that class session. You make a difference in the classroom.

Another important advantage of small classes is that you will have a chance to get to know a faculty member in a close and personal way. You will get a good insight on how faculty think and how they approach intellectual issues. You will develop a special relationship with this one particular professor because of the regular, ongoing contact.

In addition to getting to know a faculty member, the seminar also provides you with a unique opportunity to get to know your fellow college students. From your seminar conversations, you will learn about how each one thinks and how each one sees the world from a unique and special perspective. You will build close relationships with some of your classmates precisely because of your common classroom experience and the active, in-depth, and sometimes intense discussions.

Whether you are in a large public university or a smaller private college, you will have opportunities to take both large and small classes. Both types of courses certainly have value, but be sure to enroll in as many small classes or seminars as you can.

29 Immerse Yourself in Community Service

Getting involved in community work during college is important for many reasons. First, you will learn a great deal about yourself as a result of meeting and interacting with people different from you. Those contacts will cause you to reflect on yourself, your family, your racial and class background, and the privileges and challenges that you have faced in your life. Second, you will learn an enormous amount about the community with which you work in terms of the people, their racial and economic backgrounds, and the meaning and challenges they face in their lives. Third, you will begin to become a deeper thinker by beginning to see things from the perspectives of people who view the world through a different lens from yours.

These experiences are important, too, because you will be helping the community by making an important contribution. Most students don't realize just how important their impact is, whether it involves tutoring or mentoring children, visiting the elderly, or helping in an office. Community agencies depend on their volunteers' contributions, and while college students often think that what they do is inconsequential, children, seniors, and agency administrators all note the absence any time a volunteer doesn't show up when expected. It's an important lesson to realize that people depend on you and that you have a lot to offer.

In college you should recognize the distinction between community service and community service-learning. In high school, many students do community service out of a strong personal or ethical commitment, because it makes them feel good, to fulfill school requirements, or to build a good resume for college applications. What distinguishes service from service learning is that service learning requires you to read and reflect on your experience—it becomes part of your intellectual work at college in addition to service work.

What you may learn during this opportunity for reflection, first, are the many types of service and the reasons for doing it. As a Jewish student, you undoubtedly have heard many a rabbi's sermon or Hebrew school lesson about the centrality of tzedakah. Service and participation in one's community are an important part of being a citizen in a democratic society. To remain strong, democracies need their citizens to be active and involved. People do community service for a variety of reasons, ranging from how good it sometimes feels to help others, to a sense of obligation for those with more privileges to help others who are less fortunate, to religious notions of charity.

Others do community service because they feel they are partners with people from all segments of society in creating a more just society for all. They may want to go beyond being charitable to making the changes in the social structures of society that will help reduce the need for food kitchens and after-school tutors, and which will help create more jobs and better schools. These are the kinds of things you will want to reflect on in a service-learning project.

Another important lesson in service learning is the deeper understanding you will gain about social issues and identities, including social justice and the content of the service project. As a student, you will have a chance to think more about your place in society, your privileges and the challenges you face based on whether you are a member of a majority or minority social group. You will undoubtedly learn more about yourself as you learn more about the people you are serving in the community.

30 Participate in Undergraduate Research Programs

One of the best learning opportunities available to you in college is to participate directly in one of the central activities of higher education, the exploration and discovery of new ideas, new perspectives, and new knowledge. By working with faculty on their research projects, even as a first-year student, you will develop essential research skills and gain a unique insight into the world of research.

Your professors are always involved in new and ongoing research projects. Some of this research takes place in science labs, doing basic research that may eventually lead to health-related discoveries, for example. Some do computer modeling for scientific research, engineering, public policy, and economic forecasting. Other faculty conduct surveys in local communities (including the Jewish community), in hospitals, via mail or the Internet, on a national or international basis. Still other faculty do archival research in libraries, while others immerse themselves in communities to interview and observe how people live and think and to better understand the cultures of which they are a part.

Joining a research project has many benefits. First, at many colleges today, established programs will offer you course credit or work-study payment for your participation. Every student learns basic research skills in the field of the project on which they are working. Given the right circumstances, the right project, and the right set of skills, some students will have an opportunity to work with others to coauthor a research paper or to present research findings at a conference. Imagine, in your first or second year of college, having the university pay for you to travel to a conference to present your own research! You also will have a chance to get to know a faculty member and often graduate students as well, in their academic domain.

Here is how these programs often work. You must apply to under-graduate research programs. Some schools may limit participation to honors students, but this opportunity will more likely be open to any motivated student. Faculty who have volunteered to utilize under-graduates in their research will fill out information sheets about their projects, which you can then review to decide which holds greatest interest for you. You will then go interview with your top choices, and then one of the faculty, or hopefully more than one, will make you an offer to join the project.

Enjoy this wonderful learning opportunity as a young researcher!

31 Study Abroad in Israel and Other Countries

Study abroad has long been acknowledged as an important part of an undergraduate experience. In our global society today, studying abroad in Israel and elsewhere is more important than ever. Don't miss out on this learning opportunity.

Surprisingly, the number of students who go abroad during college remains relatively small, and the number who take full educational advantage of this remarkable opportunity is much smaller still.

Study abroad is important because it gives you the opportunity to both see how others live and also to see your way of life, values, studies, and national and cultural society from an entirely different perspective. You are likely to encounter new cultures, values, and foods as well as different languages, news reports, economic systems, and governmental structures. You will find that people in other countries don't always view your world or way of life as the centerpiece of how they see the world and value life.

These encounters with the new and the different and your immersion in such a society allow you to grow and learn and see much more broadly than you could ever imagine. Living and studying in another country, like other encounters with diversity, allow you to examine your life, values, and perspectives and to reaffirm, challenge, deepen, and problematize them with all the new experiences and lessons you will gather from another country.

Studying abroad can also prepare you well for a professional career that requires you to be culturally aware and sensitive to the perspectives and experiences of people living in different parts of the globe.

The most traditional approach is to go on a college-sponsored study abroad program for a semester or a year. If you go on a program that your college sponsors, it is sometimes easier to arrange credit transfer and financial aid, but a great many students go abroad on other colleges' programs and easily transfer credits and even save money. Meet with your academic advisor well in advance of your trip to make certain that your study plan will fit well with the requirements of your academic studies, and make sure to keep abreast of any safety or travel advisories.

Other ways to study abroad include summer study at various universities, theme-based programs such as theater/Shakespeare programs in England, biological/natural resources programs in Latin America, or language immersion programs in Israel or Egypt. Some students choose to pursue a semester at sea.

In recent years, even more innovative programs have emerged. Increasingly, colleges offer small groups of students an opportunity to travel abroad with a faculty member to work together on a research project or educational initiative. Other colleges now help students identify opportunities to work on a community service learning project in another country. Still other students participate in internship experiences in business, nonprofit organizations, and government agencies in various countries around the world.

This same advice applies to travel to Israel. First, yes, you should travel and study in Israel. You should also consider visiting Jewish communities in other regions of the world. Spending time in Israel will broaden and deepen your understanding of Israeli society well beyond what you have learned about Israel from your synagogues and from Jewish schools. It will strengthen your connection to Israel, Israelis, and world Jewry, and it will enable you to see the religious and social diversity of Jewish life and opinion in Israel. It will also help you to better understand the conflicted relations between Israelis and Palestinians, the tensions within Israeli society, and the critical yet complicated relations between Israeli and American Jewry. You will see the history of the Bible before your very eyes, and your Hebrew skills will improve exponentially.

There are a wide range of Israel travel and study options. Birthright Israel trips are extremely popular with Jewish students. You can also study at an Israeli university for a semester or a year. You can go on an archaeological dig, an environmental trip, or a service trip to work with communities at risk. You could study at a yeshiva, though you should check first whether your college will grant university credit, if that is a concern. You might also consider traveling to Israel to do research with a professor from your university.

It is important to think about your purpose in studying abroad. Your experience will be most beneficial and transformative if you allow yourself to meet the native residents, speak the language, and fully immerse yourself in the culture. Since many students travel on a U.S.-sponsored college study abroad program, it takes initiative on your part to avoid having an exclusively American experience even though you are in a foreign country. These students may have a great time abroad because, after all, it is fun to be on vacation, but they miss out on the deeper learning opportunity that is possible through study abroad.

Safety is certainly a consideration in travel abroad. Be sure to keep in touch with your campus study abroad office so that you are notified of any travel advisories for countries in which you wish to study.

Go study abroad, enjoy, and be safe while you experience as much as you can. Just be sure to make it a rich learning experience.

32 Learn a Second (or Third) Language, Including Hebrew

Many Jewish and other U.S. citizens wonder why there is even a need for language instruction. After all, English is spoken throughout the United States and in many parts of the world. While many Jews learn Hebrew for their Bat/Bar Mitzvah, few make regular use of the language in spoken or written form, and a minority are regular school goers. My advice to you is to stop wondering and start studying a second or third language. It's in your own best interest.

The world grows smaller and more interconnected each day. For you, as today's college student and tomorrow's professional, the nations of the globe will seem much more like the proverbial global village than anyone can begin to imagine now. Further, the multilingual global village increasingly resides not just in foreign countries but within the U.S. borders as well.

The speed of travel, the instant communication of the Internet, the rapid expansion of global business networks, and the natural resources that know no boundaries and that we increasingly share across the globe will lead us to have much more frequent and consistent contact with people everywhere. Literature, movies, politics, business, and trade cross our borders every day whether or not we choose to acknowledge the massive interdependence of the peoples throughout the world.

It has always been the case, and it is no different today, that we know we can understand and communicate better within and across cultures if we know the language of different cultures. Language in translation is considerably different and less rich than the original. The precise meanings, the cultural understandings, and the delicate nuances of language cannot be adequately captured in translation.

Your ability as an American Jew to communicate directly with Israelis in the United States or in Israel, or to read original Hebrew writing about the Middle East conflict, or to appreciate the literature and music of Israel will be greatly enhanced with a working knowledge or better of the Hebrew language. Your ability to pray with kavanah and devotion will be that much greater if you can understand the meaning of the Hebrew prayers. Traveling to Israel on a Birthright trip or a semester abroad will be that much more fulfilling if you are fluent in Hebrew.

Much of the world already speaks more than one language. As you increasingly think of yourself as a global citizen as well as a citizen of a particular nation, you will need to speak a second language to keep up. Even the United States itself is increasingly becoming a bilingual or even multilingual nation, and to move comfortably across the business and cultural sectors within this society, you should be conversant in more than one language.

When you travel abroad, you will want to speak that country's language. When you apply for a job or a promotion, you will not want to be held back because you can't speak the language of your business partners and clients. When you watch a movie, you will not want to be relegated to reading subtitles. When you read newspapers online from many different nations, you will want to read the original text. When you meet friends and colleagues from different backgrounds, you will want to freely converse and communicate deeply with them in both your and their first languages.

When you receive your college degree, you will want to think of yourself as an educated individual. Be sure to learn a second language so you will have no doubts about that claim.

4

Limud: Faculty, Classes, and Advising

33 Choose Good Teachers over Good Class Topics

Always choose the best teacher when you are planning your class schedule for the next semester. Course topics and descriptions will catch your attention, especially in college, when you will have hundreds or even thousands of courses to choose from each semester. Course topics are without a doubt important; however, a good teacher will always trump a good course title or description.

A good teacher will make any topic interesting and any course a worthwhile experience for you. You can get information and read about any topic or idea throughout your life. But a good teacher—or especially a great teacher—is a rare find, and you want to take full advantage of such an opportunity.

Good teachers force you to think and learn. They will be demanding of you, but they will be even more demanding of themselves. They will expect you to contribute to the success of the class and come to class prepared each day. They will be available and accessible to you, and they will be interested in what you are learning from the class.

Good teachers can be entertaining, but that's only occasionally the case. In fact, you should make a careful distinction between those faculty who stand out as good entertainers and those who are good teachers. Sometimes you may want to sit back in lectures and be entertained, or you may want to balance a course load with either heavy quantitative/lab or reading/writing assignments with one from another other category. Good teachers will certainly help make learning interesting, stimulating, and enjoyable, but they may not be entertainers, and they will very likely require you to work and think very hard.

When you enroll in a course whose topic you like and whose description sounds interesting, you are likely to find it to be a great learning experience. But savvy students talk with peers, older students, advisors, and even other faculty to find out more about who is teaching such an interesting topic. Some colleges post teaching evaluations of faculty and courses on student government websites. Some larger introductory courses on topics such as chemistry, statistics, psychology, and history are taught every semester by different faculty, so it makes perfect sense to wait a semester or two until you can take the subject with the best instructor.

With good teachers, you will learn new content areas, you will be challenged to think deeply, and you will be asked to examine issues analytically and from multiple perspectives. You will be expected to do your best work, and you will want to do just that because of the high standards that the professors hold for you and for themselves. You should take this opportunity to meet these professors through classroom interactions and at office hours and get to know them throughout the semester.

If you enroll in a class with a good faculty member teaching a course topic you're interested in, then you've hit the jackpot! Even for just that single course, you're going to have a terrific semester! Count on it!

34 Go to Office Hours and Get to Know Your Instructors

It is so important for you to visit your professors during office hours.

Some students are wary about going to office hours. You've been told so many stories through the admissions process about how renowned and prestigious your college's faculty are that you may feel intimidated about having a one-on-one discussion with your professor. You might be wondering why your professors would want to spend their time talking with you, a first-year student, when they have books to read, lectures to prepare, articles to write, research to complete, and other colleagues to talk with.

Most students come to office hours right after an exam to complain about their grades or to get help with what went wrong. Those are reasonable things to talk about with your professor, and you should definitely ask about what you didn't understand in an exam. However, as a general rule, they're the least interesting topics for the professor, and if that's the only time you visit, these visits are not likely to lead to building a stronger relationship. Other students come to the professor just prior to an upcoming exam or paper. That's also a good reason to speak with your professor. The only difficulty may be that if you come just before the assignment due date, then you're likely to be rushed through your meeting because you'll be waiting in line with lots of your classmates. Once again, this is another good reason to see the professor, but it won't likely be a relationship builder.

The best time to visit office hours is during those times in the semester when there is no imminent paper or exam. You should just stop by, and be prepared to ask and talk about one of the course readings or topics. If you have some background on the topic, share that with the professor. You might also want to ask the professor about his or her broader interest and experience in the field. Find out more about what professors do in their lives, what their interests are, and what projects they're currently working on.

You'll likely find that your professor will help guide this discussion and will take an interest in you. Even if it doesn't seem that way at first, you might be surprised one day when the professor stops you on the way out of class and follows up on your earlier conversation. Yes, she was really listening! If you go back to the professor's office that next week or the week after, you're likely to have twice the impact and twice the possibility of building an ongoing relationship.

You need to think of your professor's turf as your turf: the entire college is your academic learning environment, and as a member of the scholarly community, you have a right and a responsibility to feel at home in all the academic departments where you are taking classes. Faculty hold office hours precisely to meet with students in their classes; it's not the time they set aside to do research or other intellectual work. If you don't come to see your professor during office hours, he or she will still be sitting in the office alone during that time.

All faculty were college students themselves, and part of what they appreciate about their lives as professors is the opportunity to engage with interested and interesting students just like you.

35 Become Skilled at Different Ways of Knowing

As a result of your many years of schooling, you have become an expert learner—or at least you are expert in some ways of learning. College offers you the opportunity to learn in many different ways. You would do well to explore these different paths to knowledge, to gain some experience with all of them, and to identify which approaches are best suited to your learning style.

Not everyone learns in the same way. Some of your peers find sheer joy in solving mathematical problems. Others love to spend hours in the lab working on chemical experiments. A sophomore student of mine recently told me that in third grade, she was busy writing, developing, and handing out questionnaires on all sorts of topics when the other kids were playing ball at recess. What means of learning is most stimulating to you?

In college, you will find yourself in small discussion groups and in large lectures. There are benefits to both. Learn how to be an active participant in discussions and to get the most out of listening to lectures by learned scholars.

In addition to these more traditional means, some students find that they love to learn through experiential approaches. Experiential learning might mean working in an urban high school as you study about education, children, or the life of cities. It could mean designing a new traffic system as part of an engineering class. You might work in city hall on developing a new budget as part of a public policy course. Critical to experiential learning is that you take time for study and reflection about your experiences.

What are other approaches to learning that you should explore? These approaches might include discovery and exploration through research, writing a thesis, collaborative or individual projects, lernen and hevruta, and disciplinary study as well as interdisciplinary study.

High schools often emphasize one learning approach over others, and different groups of students may have been encouraged to develop their skills in certain methods and fields. For instance, men and women have traditionally had different experience with levels of encouragement in math; the same is true of white students and students of color. Regardless of your high school preparation, you should strive to gain good skills in all these areas.

Finally, you should become serious about the learning opportunities you will find outside as well as inside the classroom. Lectures, poetry readings, art exhibits, musical concerts, and theater are great learning opportunities. Participating in or becoming a leader of an organization will provide you with skills, insights, and experiences that you cannot learn through lectures or books. Internships, community service projects, acting in a play, writing for the school newspaper, producing a campus show, even working in the residence hall cafeteria or in an academic department's office are all wonderfully rich learning opportunities that you should consider.

SHIRA EISEN—*"You Mean I Can Take a Class That I'm Interested In?"*

Shira Eisen arrived at orientation with few expectations. She knew how to do well in school, but she had never been excited by any of her high school classes. Shira was aware that there were lots of requirements in college and anticipated taking the usual load of English, history, math, science, and Spanish, just as she had in high school.

It wasn't that Shira didn't have any academic interests. She loved history, but she was so tired of all those years of U.S. history. She had enjoyed science till she started her AP classes, which took so much time and always seemed more focused on what she referred to as "that stupid AP test" than on anyone learning anything interesting about science. She had liked math in middle school but was pretty much burned out from all the hours she had put in doing problem sets during high school. Spanish? Well, she was so frustrated with the attitude of her Spanish teachers in high school that sometimes she wished she had taken another language.

At summer orientation Shira met with her academic advisor, Tom, who insisted she call him by his first name. His first question was, "So, what subjects interest you, Shira?" Shira was sure this question would be shortly followed by a, "Well, that's very nice, but you'll have to wait till your junior year till you can take those courses because first you'll have to fill all your requirements." Surprisingly, though, Tom said the exact opposite. He actually encouraged Shira to take the very courses about which she was most excited. She was shocked! "When is the 'sorry, but' coming in this scenario?" she thought to herself.

Shira found an Arab-Israeli conflict poli-sci course she was really interested in and an English course that focused on women's literature. She loved the idea of taking a psychology class, but her advisor recommended instead that she do an independent research project—for credit—with a very popular psychology professor. That sounded so great! And she decided to take an environmental science class that was project-based, focusing on the health of the river that flowed along the campus outskirts.

Tom sensed her enthusiasm and suggested that they brainstorm a list of courses and projects that she might take over the next couple of years. First, Shira listed study abroad as a priority because she wanted to use the Spanish she had studied all these years, and she wanted to go on a Birthright Israel trip. Still, she wondered if she could manage going abroad for a year and still fulfill all her requirements. Shira learned that there were all kinds of study abroad opportunities. She could study abroad for a year, for a semester, or just for a summer. There were intensive language programs that lasted just one month. And her college even offered research projects organized by individual professors that lasted two to four weeks and took place abroad.

Shira had always wanted to take art history and music appreciation. She also had thought about journalism as a possible profession, and her advisor suggested that she first try writing for the school newspaper to see if she liked the field. That sounded so exciting, and apparently the newspaper accepted first year students as reporters. There were Judaic Studies courses that sounded much more interesting than anything she had learned in her Hebrew school classes. Some other science classes also sounded very interesting to her, with real-world foci on topics like AIDS, sexuality, and genetics.

Shira walked out of Tom's office so thrilled she had to pinch herself to make sure she wasn't dreaming. "I'm free!" she exclaimed to no one in particular. "This is so different from high school. I can't wait to start my classes."

36 Make Intellectual Connections among Courses

It may not count for a grade, but some of your best learning will take place when you take time to bring intellectual coherence to the wide range of courses you take each semester and each year.

A growing number of colleges are attempting to create opportunities for you to make the linkages among the seemingly disparate courses you take from the different disciplines, where you get only a sociological or biological or literary perspective. Learning communities and senior capstone courses are newer curricular efforts at many colleges to bring the importance of cross-disciplinary perspectives to bear on particular issues and topics. If your college offers these innovative programs, you should take advantage of them. If these programs are not offered, you should still try to make these linkages.

The idea is simple enough. As scholars study the complex issues of their fields and of society, it makes sense that they would want to bring to bear the full power of the intellectual perspectives and understandings of thinkers from all disciplines and departments in higher education. The same would be true in your courses. However, our colleges and universities are organized into departments according to their disciplines. Unfortunately, even though changes are beginning to take place, professors from one department commonly don't interact very frequently with their colleagues from the next department.

If you are studying environmental issues, you will need to know not only the science of the environment but also the social, political, economic, and humanistic understandings of the environment. If each of your courses focuses on just one discrete aspect of the environment, then it will be up to you to integrate the perspectives of all these fields as you attempt to better understand environmental issues. If you look at the environment only from the perspective of a biologist or an economist, you will be missing the full picture needed to make informed analyses.

If you intend to focus on the health sciences, the same is true. To better understand problems related to sexually transmitted diseases, you will want to take a wide variety of courses in genetics and the sciences, education, economics, sociology, and literature, among others. However, you will also want to do the work of making connections among what you have learned in each of these courses. Without doing so, you may become an expert in one particular area of your field, but your expertise will be narrowly tailored and limited in its impact.

This intellectual work not only will benefit your intellectual understanding of your particular field but will help to broaden your skills in doing broad multidisciplinary thinking across fields. You want to strengthen your critical thinking skills, broaden your horizons, and, at the same time, focus on a particular disciplinary area by the time you graduate. Too many students find themselves graduating with some breadth and some depth and very few if any connections among things they've learned.

Make this one of your challenges in college. Know that you can be all of these—deep, broad, analytical, and able to connect the dots across disciplinary subject fields and course topics.

You've probably been fed so many rules and instructions in your life that you can scarcely imagine that there might be any new ones you've never read. Use a #2 pencil, fill out the bubbles entirely on the standardized test, mark the answer on your chemistry exam with an X, turn in your graduation picture by the following date, use only certain margins on your research papers—you've heard it all over and over again.

I sympathize with your plight. But as you enter college, where you're considered an adult and where your decisions about courses matter and your signatures for tuition payments, housing leases, and various purchases really do have significant associated costs, now would be a really good time to start reading the instructions. And, by the way, since you've been accepted into college, no one is very patient with students who say they haven't read the rules. They know you can read!

After you've made your choice about which college to attend is a very good time to start looking more closely at the mail that comes to you. For months you've probably been immediately deleting emails and throwing out all the catalogs and form letters from all kinds of colleges, some you've never even heard of and some you probably should have applied to. But now the mail that comes is important. Be sure to send in your enrollment deposit, sign up for an orientation date, complete all your financial aid forms, return your housing lease, purchase your football tickets, and note on your calendar when you can move into your residence hall.

At orientation, you should read even more carefully. You're going to take a lot of placement tests. Be sure you fill out the answer sheets properly. Next, read the course bulletin. To be sure, it's boring. But it also serves as the college's academic contract with you. It will tell you what general education/distribution courses are required for you to graduate. It will provide you with the university calendar, so you will know when you have a fall break and when final exams and winter break are held. It will include campus maps, which, as hard as they may be to read, will come in handy on the first day of class when you're lost and need to get to a class in a big hurry.

Next, read the course guide and time schedule. Read about all the courses that are open to you, which have prerequisites and which don't, how many credits you need to complete each term, when and how often courses meet, and when final exams will be held. Check out the rules about dropping and adding classes with or without penalties, about withdrawing from school, about when tuition payments are due.

Reading instructions would certainly rank low on the list of the most intellectually liberating and stimulating tasks in college, but it will surely help you get through the logistics and bureaucracy of college life. And, that's by no means an insignificant task, so don't fight it. Read the rules, figure out the rules, learn all the angles and exceptions to the rules so you know how to use them to benefit your educational experience, and then get on with the good stuff and start having some fun learning.

38 Visit Your Academic Advisor Often

Think of your academic advisor as your coach. A coach's goal is to help you grow, improve your skills, prepare you for each upcoming challenge, and achieve your goals.

In college, the academic advisor's primary purpose is to help you succeed in your academic work. Their service and advice are free. You can visit as often as you want. At most colleges you can even change your academic advisor if you don't hit it off with an assigned advisor or if you don't believe that person is the right fit for you. What more could you ask for?

Like a coach, the academic advisor not only is looking out for you but is responsible for following the institutional rules. Your advisor will work with you to keep track of the requirements you have completed and those you still need to complete. Your advisor will want to talk with you if your grades are slipping or if you are in academic trouble.

Because some students view the academic advisor in this role as the gatekeeper and rule enforcer or as the person who intervenes only when academic difficulties arise, they maintain some distance from the advising office. That is a mistake. Remember, like coaches, academic advisors want students to succeed academically and graduate from college. Their goal is not to make problems for you.

Your advisor can give you tips on good classes to take. Advisors constantly hear from students about the quality and rigor of various courses and different faculty. They are tremendous resources. Ask them lots of questions to get the information that you feel you need to know.

What advisors like best is to think together with you about your intellectual interests, professional goals, and life commitments. They want to help you chart your own path but want you to make the decisions about what course to take or path to choose. They see themselves as facilitators. They want you to do the necessary work of identifying and clarifying your own individual desires and goals.

It's your college education, and you get to make the choices. Colleges provide you with a great resource in the form of academic advisors. They know a great deal of information that will help you make your way, and they are at your service free of charge, as often as you'd like. If academic advisors didn't exist at college, you would want to invent the idea or find someone to hire to do this very same job on your behalf. They're that valuable. Be sure to take advantage of this great resource!

39 Manage Your Time Effectively and Use a Planner

One of the most important skills you absolutely need to develop is time management. Why? Because college presents you with so much free and unstructured time that unless you know how to organize your day, you will easily and quickly get lost. It may seem like a paradox. How can it be that the more time you have, the more likely you are to find yourself running out of time?

The answer lies in the fact that most new college students have had much of the first eighteen years of their lives very structured. The arrival of college changes all that. Instead of six or seven classes that meet each day, you will probably only be taking about four classes that meet but a few times per week. Instead of having a host of after-school activities or work scheduled each day, you will have significant gaps of free time every day and throughout the day. Instead of a parent making sure you get up and go off to school in the morning or telling you to go to bed at a reasonable hour, your only reminders about going to class or going to sleep will come from yourself or your alarm clock.

So how do you go about managing your time? The first step is to use a planner and make a schedule—for each day, each week, and each month. Then you need to write the times of all your commitments, including classes, jobs, and any appointments. In the first year of college, it's also not a bad idea to write in mealtimes, because some students get so lost in their free time that they forget about meals or get too busy to find time to eat.

You should now fill in the unstructured time with estimates for study time, recreation, sleep, extracurricular activities, social functions, and even just hanging out. Be sure to fill blocks of time for both study and socializing. You will need both, and you will need limits on both so that you remain a well-rounded person.

Only you will know—and it may even take you some time to discover—how your plans work best in terms of effective study and social time. Do you need to study in short blocks so that an hour between class becomes a powerful study time when you can get a great amount accomplished? Or do you require three- to four-hour-long uninterrupted blocks of time to really focus on a topic. Maybe you need some of both to account for different kinds of assignments.

When you've been studying hard throughout the day, you'll feel good knowing that you've blocked off time on your schedule to go to a campus organization you want to explore, go for a run, or hang out on the hallway with friends.

Before you know it, your days will be filled beyond belief. You will be calling home and telling your parents that you're too busy to talk, that college assignments and expectations are greater than you ever imagined and take loads of time, that you're involved in so many exciting activities, and that your friends have come by to go down to the dining hall for dinner. Hopefully, you will have organized your schedule and learned to manage your time so that you are comfortable doing all of these wonderful things. You've learned about your study needs, and you've built a schedule that allocates plenty of time to complete your assignments but also keeps you balanced socially.

40   Go to Class on Time (and Other Rules of the High-Tech Classroom)

There is an assumption in college that you have made a deliberate and intentional decision to enter the scholarly community of higher education and that you have accepted the responsibilities that are a part of that community. This means that there is an expectation that you will behave in a respectful manner to your professors and peers and that they will be respectful toward you.

One of the delights of the college classroom, in comparison to K–12 classes, is that there are relatively few discipline problems. Students know they are in college to learn. They are there by choice, not by parental or state law, and, for the most part, they act like adult learners.

The first sign of respect is to go to class and to go on time. Particularly in a small class, you are responsible for contributing to the course's success. You cannot contribute if you do not attend. Whether you are in a small or large class, when you come to class late, you disrupt and interrupt the lecture or discussion that is in progress.

Turn off your cell phone. Don't send text messages. Don't play games on your phone. It's rude to everyone around for you to receive phone calls during class. Have you read about the safety dangers of driving while you are talking on the phone or text messaging? Doing so in the college classroom poses an equally high risk to your academic success, and to your relationship with your professor and your classmates.

Only open your laptop in class if your professor allows it. However, if your professor encourages you to take notes or to do work on your laptop during class, be sure to stick to the assignment. During class, don't play computer games or do your social networking while pretending to take notes. Would you like it if you were speaking up during class and your professor was not paying attention to you because he or she was reading email messages? You might wonder if students use the computer in class only as a result of a boring professor, but I have seen students reading newspapers, sending texts, and doing crossword puzzles during other students' presentations. It's not respectful or acceptable, so please don't allow yourself to adopt such behavior.

Don't sleep during class. If you are so tired that you can't stay awake, then you shouldn't be in class. No one wants you there when you are sleeping. Go home and go to bed.

Don't whisper to your neighbor in class. I see this behavior mostly from students who went to high school together. That they continue to behave like they were in high school is clear to everyone in the class.

If you have something so important and urgent to tell your friend that you must do so during class, then you should leave the classroom, have the conversation elsewhere, and act on the emergency you are facing. Otherwise, don't whisper.

Be a respectful learner and member of the higher education learning community. Think of your class as a community. Get yourself mentally situated to be engaged in the learning process the moment class starts. Come to class prepared. Be ready to ask questions and to offer analyses and insights. Practice good listening skills. Get to know the professor as well as your classmates.

It is a privilege to attend college. I find that first-generation college students are always among the most respectful students in class. They seem to have a special appreciation for the power and privilege that are captured in the opportunity to be part of a scholarly community at an institution of higher learning. They are joined by 98–99 percent of their classmates in that respectful behavior. Be a member of this respectful majority, and never forget how fortunate you are.

41 Read the Reading Assignments

Reading assignments represent one of the big differences between high school and college. In high school, you were tested on just about anything and everything you were assigned to read. In college, the expectation is that you will want to read everything assigned because the reason you are in college is that you want to learn as much as possible. In some cases you will be tested on reading assignments, but this is not always true. If you are tested, it will be in much more comprehensive and analytic ways.

Professors read everything they can get their hands on. They are constantly trying to get hold of the latest works in their field and beyond. When you enter their classes, especially in the first year of college, they assume—usually accurately—that you are smart and interested in the topic but know very little about the subject they are teaching. They feel compelled to load up the readings so that you can enter into the discussion of the topic. In their minds, some foundational theories, arguments, and texts are essential background information to begin the first class discussions.

You, as a typical student, are wondering if all this reading is going to be tested or if you will need to present it all back in a paper. You are thinking, based on your high school experience, that if the homework is not going to be tested or graded—and certainly if it's not going to be discussed—then there's no need for it to be assigned or for you to read it. Your professor, however, has no interest in listening to you merely repeating back the main points of this introductory material. She wants to move forward quickly to the much more nuanced literature to begin discussions in class of the more complex issues in the field.

In those subjects in which everyone has personal experience, such as family, gender relations, education, and so on, first-year students sometimes complain that the readings are just repeating the same obvious point over and over again. If you find yourself making that complaint, step back for a moment and think about how carefully you are reading the assignments. After all, your professor has spent her entire academic life reading and researching the topic you are now studying. Faculty are asking you to join them as junior colleagues, going beyond the typical surface-level understandings of the topic to the deeper and more complex layers of analysis.

As a college-educated person, you want to understand issues beyond the sound bites you hear on TV news shows or the shouting debates that pit one TV guest versus the next. Those shows give off lots of heat but shed no light and offer no insight. In contrast, the assigned readings and accompanying class discussions will take you beyond the superficial conversations to a different level.

This society needs college-educated thinkers who have the skills and understanding to analyze the most complex and vexing problems facing the world. Do the readings not as an assignment but as an opportunity to become an educated citizen, a well-informed and worldly person, and an analytic thinker. If you read and read deeply, you will begin the process of becoming one of these much needed well-educated citizens.

42 Don't Fall Behind: Learn to Be Both the Tortoise and the Hare

Time will play tricks with your mind at the start of college. You will think that you have loads of free time for studying. You will be surprised in the first weeks of the semester that some professors teaching subjects such as math and chemistry are reviewing material that you already covered in high school. You will take heart that only a few papers are required in any given social science or humanities course over the entire semester.

What's the big deal? you will think. College does not seem as difficult as you always heard about. Instead of studying, you may choose to fill your time with extracurricular activities, clubs, socializing in the residence hall, or watching lots of TV.

Then—and it will seem like it hits all of a sudden—the pace will change dramatically. The first exams will be held. The first set of papers will be due. Instead of review, your professors will begin covering new material two or three times as fast as you ever learned anything in high school. In each class you will be reading entire books in a week and multiple high-level academic articles for each class session.

How will you keep up when the semester shifts into warp speed? The answer is simple. You will need to have the best traits of both the tortoise and the hare. You need to be steady and consistent in your study habits, ready for the long haul of the semester. At the same time, you need to be ready for the bursts of energy required when there is an especially heavy load of tests or papers any given week. That won't happen often, but it will happen, so it's best to keep yourself in good mental and physical health for those times when you need to set everything aside to get all your work done.

The key is to always keep up with your work, even when the workload seems light. Falling behind and catching up later should not be an option. Trust me on this one—it won't work. By keeping up with your work, you will be in good shape when a rush of assignments from multiple classes are all due at once. It will allow you flexibility for those times when you catch a cold, have heavy extracurricular commitments, or something very exciting comes up spontaneously.

Keep in mind that generations of college students have been able to keep up with the heavy workload. You very clearly have all the intellectual ability and schooling experience not only to keep up but to excel in all your subjects. Just remember to be both the tortoise and the hare, and don't let yourself fall behind.

SAM BERGMAN—*"I've Got So Much Free Time!"*

Sam Bergman's course schedule was made in heaven. No Friday classes. Mondays and Wednesdays he had class from one o'clock to four o'clock, and Tuesdays and Thursdays he had class from ten to twelve and four to six. Sam figured he could sleep late every day, start his weekend partying on Thursday night, and pretty much play around much of the semester. When he moved into his room at the start of the semester, he spent a lot of time setting up his home theater system to get the best sound imaginable for his music and high-def TV.

Sam started the semester sleeping late and staying up to all hours of the night. He planned to do his homework Sunday afternoons but ended up watching football. Monday and Wednesday mornings were open times for study, but he usually got up too late to get anything useful done. His best study time was between class on Tuesdays and Thursdays, from twelve to four, but in reality it was one to four, because he liked to talk with his friends leisurely over lunch. Friday afternoon was supposed to be another study time, but he was usually already in the weekend party mode by that time.

Sam was a smart guy, and he thought he could keep up with his studies pretty well. He did the bare minimum, which always did the trick in high school. But he quickly found out that this wouldn't work in college. On his first paper, he got a C– with some pretty harsh comments from his professor. His first chemistry exam resulted in an E.

Sam was already heavily involved in his fraternity rush activities. Since he always seemed to be available, the frat brothers began to call on him to help with parties and other activities during the week and on weekends. Sam loved that he was so popular in the college fraternity and that he could keep up with the best of the partiers and drinkers, even those who were juniors and seniors. He often hung out till three in the morning in the frat house, talking and drinking with the guys and doing various chores.

One of Sam's professors contacted him about his grades and told him to come to office hours. Sam was in major denial about his academic work and felt like he didn't have to respond to the professor. But this professor kept after him and insisted he stay after the next class to talk with her. She questioned him about his unsatisfactory work and about his obviously disinterested body language in class. She told him that he would fail the course if his work didn't significantly improve. Sam was slightly embarrassed at this conversation and told her he'd try harder.

Two weeks later he failed another test, this one in Spanish. Sam's Spanish teacher sent him an email requesting to speak with him. Sam was impressed that people were taking an interest in him, but he also felt humiliated, like a little schoolboy being sent to detention. However, this professor, unlike the first, challenged him about his party habits and asked whether he had an alcohol problem. He even asked whether Sam was hoping to fail—maybe he didn't really want to be in college and would prefer to take a year off.

Sam was kind of stunned to be having these conversations with his college professors. That night he called a close friend from home whom he hadn't talked with since the first week of school. He shared what had happened. His friend was understanding but also very honest in expressing his disappointments about Sam's behavior and approach to college. Sam began to wonder what had gone wrong for him.

Sam made a commitment to himself to get back on track. He met with his academic advisor to map out a strategy. To his surprise, even the advisor questioned whether Sam wanted to withdraw from the semester altogether because it would be so difficult to dig himself out of this hole. His advisor also referred him to a personal counselor, saying that if he were serious about his studies, he would first have to get more serious about getting his life back on track.

In the end, Sam passed his courses that term with a C– average. He worked out a very detailed schedule—day by day, hour by hour—of study time, class time, and some time for fun. He realized that what he had written off as free time in his high school mind-set was really meant to be study time in college. There really was no other way around it. Sam started going to counseling about his drinking and his overall attitude, and he cut way back on his fraternity activities. Some of the brothers were critical and gave him a hard time, but others really supported him in getting his priorities in order. Sam's professors commented on his changed attitude and performance, but it was a major shock to him to get final grades of Cs and Ds instead of As and Bs.

When Sam came home for winter break, he spoke honestly with his parents for the first time and told them that he had done poorly in his first semester of college. Sam's parents were disappointed, angry, and concerned. They offered their support and help, but Sam could tell he had lost some of their respect. Sam said he had learned a lot about the need to find balance in his life.

It took another semester of time management advice and low grades before Sam really did get his priorities in life in order. He realized that he truly hadn't been ready for the demands of college that year. He was certainly smart enough, but he hadn't been ready for the freedoms he had been given in terms of free time and independence. He may not have gotten good grades that year, but he sure learned a most important lesson that would serve him well throughout his life.

43 Think Sensibly and Strategically about Grades

How should you think about grades in college? Grades are such an overriding concern for most high school students because of the tremendous pressures to gain admission to the college of their choice. But what happens to grades in college?

Let's first do the mathematics of college grades. The most traditional college plan would have you take an average of four courses each semester, attend two semesters of college each year, and go to college for four years. That comes to 32 classes. Thus, the final grade for each class you take counts only about 3 percent of your final college grade point average. In each class, you will have an average of four assignments/exams that comprise your grade. If each of these assignments were weighted equally, then each would be worth less than 1 percent, or .75 percent, of your final college grade point average.

Keep the above calculations in mind when you get your first grades on papers or tests in your first semester of college. If you get your first ever C on your first exam—and many students do get lower-than-expected grades on their first papers and exams—use it as a learning experience about the difference between high school and college expectations for quality of work and the necessity of good study skills. But don't panic about it being a career-ending signal. That C you received counted only .75 percent of your final college GPA. It didn't rule you out for a career in medicine, law, or teaching or for doctoral studies in biology or sociology.

Some students vociferously argue about getting an A– grade rather than an A. If you think your professor made a mathematical error or some other clear and legitimate mistake in your grade, bring it to his attention. Otherwise, just forget about it. Relax. An A– grade means you were nearly excellent in your work in that course. Feel good about your accomplishment.

If you think you deserve an A on a paper because your high school teacher praised your writing and your college professor has numerous suggestions on how you can improve, please don't complain. What you need to do, instead, is adjust your expectations and raise your own standards. If you believe you need an A to get into business school, don't think your sense of entitlement will go very far with your professor.

Grades can still be meaningful in college, but their meaning is quite different. On the one hand, if you are applying to certain professional schools, like medicine or law, your GPA along with standardized test scores will certainly be one of the important admissions criteria. On the other hand, if you are applying to graduate programs, while grades are considered, there will be less attention to insignificant grade differentials, such as whether you received a 3.8 or a 3.7 GPA. Faculty letters of reference, special accomplishments in the discipline, and work or research experience in the field will often carry considerable weight in conjunction with the more traditional measures. If you plan to go out and look for a job after you receive your B.A., few employers will look closely or exclusively at your grade point average.

However, there is a marked ranking difference in terms of the value of the degree for students who plan to pursue advanced degrees. Clearly, those who receive a 3.5 GPA or higher are in a far stronger position than those who graduate with a 2.5 GPA or lower. In this sense, grades do matter significantly. But they shouldn't matter to the extent that you focus on grades more than you focus on learning or that you lose any of the joy of the college experience for the achievement of a high grade point average. Further, they shouldn't cause you to worry endlessly about any single low grade you receive.

Many faculty wish they didn't have to grade; they would prefer to give students careful feedback and not just a letter grade with all the baggage that a grade carries. Other faculty do believe it's important to sort out students, particularly in larger introductory classes, in order to give students a realistic assessment of their capabilities for graduate study in certain professional fields. Faculty approaches to grading vary across fields of study, and faculty themselves disagree with one another about issues of grade inflation.

Think about how you want to approach the issue of grades in college. Most important, don't let your good grades interfere with your learning.

44 Don't Freak Out over Finals

You've taken tests and written papers throughout your twelve or more years of prior schooling. You've obviously done fairly or very well on those exams in order for you to have been admitted to college. In all likelihood, you've also taken final exams for at least a few years. If you take a moment to think about it, you have as much experience in test taking as you do in almost any aspect of your life. Consider yourself an expert!

As the last weeks of the semester approach, there's always a buzz on campus about finals. "How many finals do you have?" "Are they spaced out over several days or bunched together?" "I hear that professor gives really hard finals." "I have only one final, but I've got three long papers due." "I've got to get at least a B on my final to get a decent grade." You should rise above this unfortunate level of anxiety that spreads through campus about finals.

You know how to do this. You make a finals schedule, a study guide for each class, and a study schedule to go with it. You figure out where you want to study—your room, the library, a lounge, an empty classroom. You arrange for study groups or you prepare by yourself. You review your notes, go over the texts, identify key themes, topics, information. You stay healthy by eating right and getting enough sleep. You reserve some free time to relax. You get to the exam a few minutes early, take a deep breath, complete the final, and give a sigh of relief.

If it's that easy, why does it seem so hard? The hardest part is psychological. While there is an elevated level of anxiety on campus about finals, it is still within normal limits. Where there is an unhealthy degree of anxiety, even a degree of frenzy, is in your college home, your residence hall. If you were in an apartment or house on campus, you'd be living with three or four others who had varying degrees of anxiety about their finals, just as they might about any exams. In the residence hall, however, and particularly in residence halls where most first-year students live, there's a fabricated and unhealthy level of anxiety because everyone around you—thirty, fifty, two hundred, or even a thousand students—is about to take his or her first set of college final exams.

All around you people are talking about their upcoming finals. It might be fun at first to have this shared experience, but it quickly becomes annoying and distracting, and it can also be unhealthy. The residence halls try their best to address the situation with round-the-clock quiet hours, study breaks, snacks, and various other distractions.

What you need to remember is that a final exam is just an exam. Be smart by anticipating that there will be a heightened degree of anxiety in the residence hall. Know that it's coming, but don't let it affect you. Focus on your studies, not the anxieties in the air. Eat well. Get rest. Avoid the all-nighter if at all possible. However, if you should feel overwhelmed at any point, go to the campus counseling office, where there are almost always extra staff on duty, walk-in appointments, and people ready to assist and support you at this point in the semester. Finals go by very quickly, and before you know it you'll be at home for a few days of work, rest, relaxation, and a much-needed change of pace.

45 Be Intellectually Honest: Don't Cheat

At college it's called "academic integrity." It is the academic equivalent of civil law. Academic integrity is essential to the entire enterprise of scholarly inquiry and intellectual exploration.

In college, cheating is like stealing. If you are caught cheating, you will be brought before an academic judiciary. You will face punishment that can range from a stern warning to a failing grade on a test or entire course, suspension, or expulsion.

The best and only advice about cheating is to never, ever do it.

Your purpose in college is to learn, and you will learn nothing from cheating. You are stealing someone else's ideas in order for you to get a better grade.

There are many views as to why a significant amount of cheating occurs on college campuses. Some people believe it just reflects the breakdown of basic values in society, a lack of respect for rules, peers, and authority. Others suggest that there is so much stress and competition to get top grades, particularly in the preprofessional programs, that students feel pressured to break the rules in order to fulfill their professional goals. Finally, some students unknowingly cheat, not being fully aware of what constitutes plagiarism.

Students cheat (and get caught) in any number of ways. They look over a classmate's shoulder during an exam to get an answer. They copy other students' papers. They buy papers over the Internet. They use pieces of other people's works without giving any citation. They set up computer programs to use other people's work to complete lab assignments and math problems. Faculty and university administrators know all the tricks of the trade and are quite adept at identifying student cheaters.

The question of academic integrity is a matter of personal integrity. The cheating habits you develop or maintain in college are likely to stay with you throughout your business life and personal relations. If you cheat because you feel unbearable stress in college, rest assured that the pressure will be that much more intense and stressful in the work world. Don't get started down this wrongheaded path. You are better than this. You don't want or need to get ahead by cheating.

Live your life honestly so you can wake up every morning proud of your life and proud of all your accomplishments. Examine your ethical makeup and your personal integrity. Set yourself on the right course in college, and it will serve you well throughout your entire life.

46 Take Full Advantage of Learning Opportunities as a Commuter Student

If you are a commuter student, will you still have an opportunity to get to know faculty, attend office hours, meet your peers for study groups, hang out after class to discuss class topics, and attend cocurricular lectures, speakers, and political debates? The answer is yes, you will certainly have that opportunity, but you must be assertive to make sure it happens.

One of the best ways to take advantage of all your learning opportunities is to participate in a learning community. The learning community will provide you with a group of students who are eager to engage with one another and build friendships around intellectual ideas and academic projects. It will also introduce you to faculty who seek to mentor and get to know students in a more individual and personal way.

Many faculty hold office hours immediately before or after classes meet. Therefore, you should plan to come to class early or leave later after class in order to meet with your professors during office hours. Build office hour time into your regular commuting schedule rather than having to make all sorts of special travel arrangements when there is a problem at hand and you have no choice but to see your teacher.

Similarly, if your schedule permits, plan on staying on campus later one or two days each week. Campus talks and speakers usually take place late in the afternoon or early evening. Try to leave some designated time in your campus schedule to make your attendance at these events an occasional or even routine occurrence. Study groups will usually take place in the evening, so by leaving an evening free you will be able to participate with your classroom peers in these important study sessions. In addition to focusing on the specific topic at hand, study groups always lend themselves to discussion of a wide range of topics related to your class discussions. These gatherings will give you access to the valuable learning that also takes place in the informal spaces of college when students just hang out together.

It's more difficult but not impossible by any means to be fully involved in the college scholarly community as a commuter student. You just need to be organized at home, at work, and at college and to manage your time effectively. Be sure that your plan as a college student is not to just take courses but to be an engaged learner—engaged with your texts, your professors, and your fellow students. Doing this will increase your satisfaction with your college experience and should benefit your academic success at college.

47 Return to the Three Rs— Reading, 'Riting, and 'Rithmetic

Now that you've been admitted to college, you may be feeling both very confident in your academic abilities and at the same time embarrassed that you still need help with some of the basic foundational learning skills. I find that far too many students, both those from weak high schools as well as those from high schools considered in the top 10 in the country, still need some instruction and support in one or more areas of the "basics." Be sure to get this additional instruction and support.

Even more distressing than the fact that too many students have inadequate skills in the basics is that there is shame associated with it. Students far too often will try to hide their lacking skills in these areas, and faculty far too often do not challenge students to get the instructional support they need.

You can learn all of these skills. And, because you are in college, almost all of which have numerous kinds of academic resource centers and support services, you have an absolutely unique opportunity to learn these skills and get good control of them. Don't try to use your smarts to hide your inadequate high school training: Get assistance! After you graduate from college, you will never have the chance or inclination to go back to these areas of inadequate skills. And, if you feel bad enough now to hide these skill problems, you will feel that much worse after college. Now is the time!!

Why haven't you learned these skills? In some cases, even though you are a very bright person and outstanding student, your K–12 schools have been inadequate and have not provided the basic foundational needs you require in a whole range of areas. In other cases, educational policy in some well-intentioned schools has probably tipped too far to emphasize broader themes of learning and the basic skills have not received sufficient emphasis.

My advice to all of you who find yourself in this situation is to drop any low self-image or embarrassment for needing help with this. This is not a test of your intellectual ability—these are skills! Give yourself an emotional break with this.

Go online or talk to your advisor, your professor, or your friends and find out where the academic resource center is located. Set up a first appointment and plan on coming back for an entire semester. More than likely it will take some time to fully learn these skills.

Finally, go on with your life and enjoy! Know that you're going to do great work in college and beyond.

5

Tikkun Olam: Make a Difference in the World

48 Live a Life of Commitment: Take Responsibility for the World around You

You bring a new set of eyes to the world around you. As a college student, you have the ability to see problems and opportunities that older people may not see so clearly. Each generation has the chance—even the responsibility—to learn from the past and present and to make changes to improve and sustain society for the future. This isn't a frivolous responsibility; it is one you should accept with respect, courage, and commitment.

College is a time when you get to think a lot about yourself—your development and growth, your personal ambitions, your relationships, and your academic success. It is actually quite important that you take the time necessary to think hard about the kind of person you want to be as an adult.

At the same time, it's just as important that you begin to see yourself as someone who can and should make a significant impact on the world around you. Just as there is a value in looking after your own well-being, as citizens of our communities, cities, nations, and world, we also need to look after the well-being of those around us.

There is, in fact, a long tradition in the Jewish community, and in the United States and elsewhere, of college students asking hard questions of college and political leaders about societal conditions. Those questions have often been linked to student activism and to taking a stand for moral principles.

There are a number of ways to think about this social responsibility. First, taking responsibility for others is a sign of moving from childhood, when you are the responsibility *of* others, to adulthood, when you are responsible *for* others. Second, taking responsibility for other people and for societal issues is a positive sign of empowerment, indicating that you consider yourself a full-fledged member of society and that you feel you have the motivation and power to actually contribute to the well-being of others and to create change in society. Third, it demonstrates that you have enough confidence in yourself to give of yourself to others.

How might you take responsibility for the world around you? There's a whole range of approaches, and you should find the ways that best fit your personality. One way to do this is through your personal relationships: how you relate to acquaintances, friends, even strangers. Do you interrupt homophobic or anti-Semitic jokes, do you behave respectfully toward the man or woman with whom you develop a romantic relationship, do you speak openly and honestly about people around you just as you would if they weren't present?

Others may find that they can give back to society most constructively through community service and volunteer work, by tutoring in a school, by volunteering in a hospital, through philanthropy, or by serving in an organization and on its committees. Still others decide to run for political office, to vote in elections, to write letters to the editor, or to contest college administrators' or political leaders' decisions.

Decide what approach best fits who you are. This process may take some time, but look at the world around you and work to make it a better place than when you entered it.

49 Think about Social Justice

Have you ever thought about what you would do if you had the power to make the world a better place? You should give this some consideration during your college years because you'll find that you have much more power to influence change than you might imagine.

When people talk about social justice, issues such as hunger, homelessness, health care, and discrimination often come to mind. What areas do you think need change to create a more just world for everyone?

While it may not be difficult to identify the many areas that need change, the reasons for injustices and the solutions for creating more just conditions are often very complex. Sometimes the problem is as simple as bad people doing bad or even horrific things to others. Usually, however, the problem lies in the historic and structural conditions that maintain inequalities and injustices within societies or across national borders.

As a person embarking on a college education, you will have an opportunity to investigate and better understand the underlying causes of injustice in the world. It may be frustrating, to some extent, to learn how difficult it is to find comprehensive solutions. However, your new knowledge and insights may empower you to take action to work for the changes necessary to bring about a more just society.

One of the lessons you will learn in your studies is how powerful a person you are, in relative terms, just because you've received a college education. Globally, your college education places you among an elite group in the world. This is a privilege and opportunity you should not take lightly.

You might wonder how you could be a member of an elite group when you look about and see so many with so much more than you have. Surprisingly, sometimes it's precisely when we do have power and influence that we don't realize what we have.

Your college education gives you rights and responsibilities that comparatively few people worldwide possess. While you may be thinking that you're not so exceptionally smart or privileged given your place in your high school class rank or the fact that you may not have gained admission to your first-choice college, the fact of the matter is that you are among the most highly educated people in the world.

Think about what good you want to do with your education. What does social justice mean to you? What can you do to make a change in the world, whether it be among your friends and family, Jews and non-Jews in your community, your city, your state, or your nation or across national borders? How can you take advantage of the power and privilege that your college education confers to make the world a more just place for everyone?

50 Take Democracy Seriously: Participate Actively in Civic Life

Those of us who have grown up in a democratic society often assume that our way of government will go on forever and ever. But a growing chorus of scholars warns that democracies are actually fairly fragile enterprises that may not endure unless they are cared for and looked after.

That's our job, and that's your job.

Here is a list of things you can do to make your democracy stronger and enhance your college experience and the reasons why these activities are so important. Remember, our democracy is of the people, by the people, and for the people—and you are the people!

Vote! When only a few people vote, it means that a small elite is getting to make the decisions for you about who runs our cities, our states, and our country. That's not very democratic.

Get involved and participate! Run for office in your student government. Attend a city council meeting and voice your opinion. Go to your town's school board meetings. Write a letter to the editor of your newspaper. Fewer and fewer citizens are involved in local politics. Again, that means that a small minority are making decisions about how we should live our lives!

Join organizations! You don't need to be political, but you need to be involved in the community. Join a student club, an environmental organization, a hiking and camping group, a choir, a sports team, a religious or ethnic group, or a social organization. Citizen involvement in community organizations and clubs has dropped sharply; instead, people are sitting home alone watching TV or spending more time at work. An engaged citizenry makes for a strong democracy by sharing news, discussing ideas, and building community.

Do community service! Make the concerns of your neighborhood and surrounding towns and cities your business. Yes, it does take all of us to keep the nation's democracy healthy and vibrant for this generation and those to follow. If we don't care about the people in our community, state, and nation, we can't expect that elected officials will care about you or your neighbors. Citizens in a democratic nation look after other citizens and take responsibility for the good of the whole.

Get a good education! Democracies need educated citizens—citizens and leaders who can think critically, reason analytically, and size up complex problems from many different perspectives. An uneducated, uninformed citizenry is more likely to follow demagogues and fail to challenge bad ideas from wrongheaded leaders. College students like you, who will be well educated and involved in society, are our nation's best hope for a strong, diverse democracy.

ALEX BROOKS—*"Stepping Outside My World"*

Alex Brooks chose his college for two reasons: (1) it has a great academic reputation, and (2) it is a distance from his home and has a much more diverse student body than his suburban community. Alex grew up in a bedroom community outside a big city, surrounded by Jewish white, middle-class students like himself. His parents were happily married and worked, his dad as a broker and his mom as an accountant.

Alex was very popular and loved his hometown, but he also read a lot and knew that there was a bigger world outside the comfort of his home. He was among the first in his town to attend this particular college, and it hadn't been an easy decision for him. It took some courage to leave behind the safety of familiar friends and neighbors to explore the world through college.

When Alex arrived at college, he was so pleased to meet people from different states, different religions, and different racial and ethnic backgrounds. That's what he had been looking for. But, despite everyone's initial friendliness, there seemed to be an element of superficiality to all the friendliness. Oh, everyone was nice enough, really, but Alex didn't feel particularly welcome at some of the events that were held for other students, like the Black orientation, the Pan-Asian barbeque, or the Christian student movie night.

Alex went to Hillel Shabbat on Sunday and felt at home in the service, though he did miss his synagogue at home. He also decided to participate in fraternity rush in order to make some close friends. All of this provided some comfort to Alex, but he was aware that his friends were all like the ones he knew at home. All were white, all were middle-class, all were Jewish.

One day, a close friend from home, Mark, made a comment that took Alex by surprise: "Why did you go so far away to college if you were just going to hang around with all the same kind of people like back here at home? Maybe you should come back home where your best friends are and think about transferring to the prestigious college in the city."

That comment shocked Alex. Wow! Alex felt really close to Mark and other friends from home, but he had no intention of leaving his college. That wasn't at all what he wanted. It wasn't as if Alex didn't want to have all the good friends he had made, but Mark's comment was a reminder that Alex really did want to meet new friends, including students from many different backgrounds. That was, in fact, one of the important reasons why he had chosen this school. College, he had always believed, was about meeting the world—not just in books but in the diversity of the campus. Still, Alex wondered how he was going to meet any of these new people.

Over the next few weeks, Alex made a point of reaching out and extending himself. Although it felt awkward and uncomfortable to him, he sat down at a lunch table in the residence hall cafeteria with a few of the African American students that he had met at orientation. Without hesitation, they included him in their conversation about classes. When the Asian-American students on his floor were talking about a party they planned to go to that weekend, he asked if he could join them, and they were happy to have him along. Even though a Hillel group was getting together to watch the college's football game, Alex decided to stay in the residence hall to watch it at the party the hall council had organized, and he was thrilled to see all the different groups of people gather together to support the team.

As Alex took these steps to branch out, he also found himself trying other new activities. He went to the mass meeting for students wanting to try out for the school newspaper. He attended an evening lecture on the role of business in foreign affairs. He talked to one of his professors to see if he could help him out with his research project on health care in Latin America.

What really thrilled Alex as he reached out and experimented with these new friends and opportunities was that he found that he hadn't had to give up his Jewish traditions or practices to be with others. In fact, his friends from other religions asked if they could come join him when he went to schul at Hillel on Friday nights and Saturday. His new friends from the Philippines and Chile wanted to know all about his own ethnic and religious heritage. Alex had long talks with a friend whose parents were divorced, with guys who came from very wealthy families, and with students who worked twenty-five hours a week and even then barely kept up with school loans.

Alex found what he was looking for in college. He hadn't lost the comfort and safety of his Jewish home and neighborhood, his own bubble; rather, he had found that he could also have safety in a much wider comfort zone. He didn't have to choose one or the other but settled into a fulfilling and meaningful life in a much bigger world than his hometown had allowed. Alex had made the right choice for himself.

51 Be Both an Activist and a Thinker

Make a commitment to yourself to be a thinking person who will make a difference in the world.

Be a thoughtful agent for social change and social justice, regardless of your political perspective. Develop a passion for involvement and participation that is based on the analytical tools, complex thinking skills, and knowledge learned in your classes.

It's not enough to be just a good thinker or just an activist. You need to be both. You need to learn to apply your thoughtfulness into good practice.

American colleges have a long history of youthful activism. That history is to be celebrated because a democratic society needs dedicated, involved, caring people who are passionate about the pressing issues in their society.

At the same time, that history of activism has also been marked on occasion more by action than by thoughtful analysis. This society and the world at large have little need for stone-throwing students, riots over sporting victories, or yet more simplistic solutions to the complex problems facing the globe.

An increasing number of today's student activists have been trained by well-organized national, governmental, and global agencies to advocate on campus for particular viewpoints. I find this to be a very disappointing trend because these students, however well-meaning, are merely repeating slogans and reproducing documents fed to them by high-priced marketing professionals. What they are doing is the opposite of independent and critical thinking.

You need to be a student who thinks for yourself. Listen to others' points of views, attend lectures, conferences, and information sessions, and read voraciously, but don't become just another ideologue. Your ability to think independently and to bring nuanced, critical reasoning to enormously complex problems is precisely what the world is hoping you will learn to do with your college education. Don't go the simplistic, sound-bite, PR-managed, propaganda route.

Don't assume there is only one right position or room for a debate between just two parties. There may be multiple truths to consider and multiple voices that need to be heard. Where it appears that no solution is to be found or that no one is standing up for what you believe, then take responsibility for finding that solution and standing up for yourself.

Society needs your thoughtful, well-researched, and considered perspective on all matters of public interest. Be sure you speak up so we can all learn from you and so that you make this world a better place for everyone to live in.

52   Withhold Assumptions about People

You walk onto campus and you see someone looking at you. You've never met this person, but you can tell that he or she is sizing you up. This person is drawing a mental picture of who you are, putting you into a small and limiting box.

No one would question that he or she is drawing a distorted, stereotypical picture of you. At the same time, the truth is that almost all of us do the same kind of sizing up of other people around us, making judgments and drawing on social constructions and stereotypical images of all kinds of unique individuals around us.

Especially for the many students (which includes most Jewish students) who come from homogeneous backgrounds, the stereotyping and dismissal of people based on physical characteristics represents a tremendous opportunity lost. A woman with blond hair—haven't we been taught throughout our lives a negative, stereotypical image about that person's intelligence? A man with an earring—is that truly supposed to give us clear insight into that person's personality and values? A southern accent in a northern state or vice versa—do any of us really believe that we can learn anything substantive about someone's personality from an accent?

And yet so many college students are inclined to go ahead and forge friendships with or avoid people based on these grand assumptions based on so little (mis)information. Some of us will set high or low expectations of people based on what region of the country they come from. "Oh, you're from New York? Or Chicago? Well, I've got you all figured out. I know what you're all about." Surely, if we paused for just an instant, all of us would know that this one person cannot possibly be exactly like the other millions of people in New York City.

So what's the problem? The problem is that when others do this to us or we do the same to others around us, we lose sight of the very special, unique characteristics that each of us prides ourselves on as individuals. We erase the individuality and soul of each person around us. And, as is usually the case, we miss out on opportunities to meet all kinds of amazing people.

The sad part is that far too many of your fellow college students may be judging you in the same way. How wrong and simplistic can they be! Yet all these college students are supposed to be so smart!

My hope is that you will be just a little bit smarter than they are. Try this. Every time you meet a new person at college, withhold your assumptions about them. Try to actually meet and get to know the person behind the handbag, the t-shirt, the skin color, the city they come from, the accent, or the weight and height. Get to know each person's individual values, history, aspirations, humor, and friends. Find out about others just as you'd hope they would want to learn about you.

I think this approach not only will give you a chance to make real, lasting friendships with people from all backgrounds but along the way will help you to learn to like yourself a lot more as you give yourself and others a chance to grow beyond the little boxes into which we paint ourselves.

53 Be a Boundary-Crosser: Dialogue and Engage with Others

The next generation of leaders will be boundary-crossers. You should learn to be one as part of your college education.

Boundary-crossers can move easily across groups and categories of people. They have the attitude, skills, and mind-set that allow them to transcend the social barriers that most people don't dare cross.

Boundary-crossers are respectful of other people and are interested in their commonalities and differences. They are good listeners but are just as willing and ready to fully engage. They are open and honest.

Boundary-crossers see connections and opportunities for collaboration. They are expert at linking people together locally, nationally, and globally. They don't see walls, they see pathways.

Boundary-crossers are comfortable with people, ideas, and organizations. They have a natural curiosity about all kinds of subject matter, and they find people's lives and stories intriguing. They are problem-solvers, connectors, and bridge-builders. They don't need to be at the top of the hierarchy, but we'd all be a lot better off if more of them were. They can move easily across the different ranks of personnel within an organization.

As a college student, you can both learn the skills of boundary-crossers and practice those skills. By intentionally working to expand your comfort zone, you will begin to gain a level of ease being with people from different social backgrounds. By getting to know the persons behind particular viewpoints, you will appreciate how even well-educated, well-meaning, and very likeable people can differ dramatically on politics and issues of intellectual interest. By taking a broad array of courses across various disciplines, you will gain an understanding about why and how different people can be so intrigued by and even passionate about topics that you hadn't even heard of.

In college you will find the same walls set up to divide people and organizations that exist in society at large. Students will divide themselves up by social identity groups. Those students with different political views from their neighbors won't associate with each other except to shout their views louder than the next person. Student leaders of one organization won't even think of the opportunities that exist by collaborating with the organization next door, let alone acting in anything but a competitive manner.

You can be different. You can bring people and organizations together. You can be friends with individuals from different political parties and religions as easily as you can be friends with people who represent different racial groups or who have different majors. You can engage your peers regarding contentious issues but still leave the discussion with respect for one another. You can find common ground and opportunity in difference.

In becoming a boundary-crosser, you will find that your learning increases exponentially by moving across and between boundaries. You will find that your friendships are as wide as they are deep. You will learn to see value and opportunity in almost every person, idea, issue, and organization you encounter. You will be prepared to take on leadership roles in your family and community. In civic life, in business, and throughout your professional life, you will be a much-sought-after person. You will see the world more positively, and you will make the world a more positive place in which to live.

Kids have opinions from a very young age, and they know how to express themselves. Though it's usually about very personal issues—needing a nap, wanting a diaper changed, being hungry—they're quick to let you know what they're thinking.

Over the next eighteen years, however, through parenting, schooling, and other socializing institutions, children and especially teenagers are taught not to have their own opinions. They're told it's rude to disagree with an adult. Their teachers tell them over and over again not to invoke a personal view into papers or to use the first person *I*. The first person is essentially prohibited in most high schools—no *I*, no opinions, no viewpoint, no personal positions—leave that to the adults, the teachers, the experts.

Along comes college, and suddenly professors are asking you for your opinion and expecting you to have one! "How does your personal experience inform the theory of this author?" your professor will ask. You will be asked to write in the first person. You will be challenged to rediscover the *I* in your vocabulary and thought processes.

As you walk across the college campus, students will confront you about your views on the upcoming election—who are you voting for, and why? They will want to know your opinion about foreign affairs and your stand on Israel. They will ask you to join a demonstration for or against a civil rights issue. You will be invited to a talk by a conservative or liberal speaker and will be expected to know who the speaker is and whether you support his or her view or not.

You will be asked about religion—about Judaism, about organized religious institutions, and more generally about faith and spirituality. You will be questioned about the ethnic joke or gender joke you make at someone's expense. It may have sounded funny and harmless at the high school lunch table, but now, in college, you may be challenged to consider and defend the sensibility of that humor.

There will be campus issues you'll be expected to think about, too. Is tuition too high? Should there be a student-run bookstore? Do you support a "safe walk" program on campus? Should professors give final exams before the last day of class? What hours should be set for quiet time on your residence hall floor? Should the cafeteria offer whole wheat bread or white?

You know and believe that Israel is a foundation of Jewish history, religion, and culture. As a Jewish student, you will be confronted by Jews and non-Jews alike with strong opinions and with difficult and pressing questions about the State of Israel. "What are your views of the current peace process in Israel?" "Do you support Israel's governmental policies 100% and are you prepared to publicly defend them?" "What are your views of Palestinian rights?" "Are you planning to attend this speaker's talk, are you going to this student organization's political protest, are you planning to go to the opposing group's political demonstration?"

These questions may seem overwhelming and yet very exciting at the same time. What if you don't know enough to have an informed opinion? How do you learn about these things? What if you don't care or never cared before? What if you care really deeply and want to become a leader of one of these groups?

There are loads of sound-bite answers to complex questions in society that truly require clear, critical, and complex answers. As a college-educated person and as a Jew, you will want to understand the complexities of issues and to arrive at answers that go beyond traditional, simplistic solutions. The starting point is to realize that your opinion matters and that society and the Jewish community need you to have that informed opinion. Don't let others form your views for you. Your view and your voice matter.

ADAM KAPLAN—*"I've Got an Opinion about That!"*

In Adam Kaplan's home, his father set the rules. He was a man of strong values and a strong will, and when it came to Arab-Israeli issues, no one was about to challenge him. And, with such a strong adult in the house, no one ever thought about asking Adam for his opinion.

Sometimes, however, Adam rebelled against his father because he got tired of his father always thinking he was right, and the two of them had at times exchanged some strong words. For Adam, it hardly mattered to him what his father said or what they were fighting about; although the argument was usually about Israel, he just got into the habit of being contrary, especially with his father. So Adam came to college with a penchant for rebelling and arguing when the mood hit him.

Adam was amazed the first day he passed through the campus commons. Students were passing out flyers and speaking through megaphones about all kinds of issues and the Israel debate was right in the middle of it. They seemed just like his dad—strident, self-assured, strong willed, and completely certain they were 100% right. Adam hated their cockiness but kept his mouth shut—after all, he was just a first-year student.

But Adam kept meeting students who felt so strongly about all kinds of issues. There was something stimulating about the debates and the issues. Although Adam didn't really know too many of the issues, he knew from his fights with his father (and similar contrarian behavior in public school and Sunday school) that he could be a pretty strident critic of others' viewpoints.

Adam decided to enter the fray one day while he was passing through the commons. As one student was loudly exhorting the students going by on their way to class, Adam paused and let the student know how stupid he thought his views were. Rather than act defensively, which was what Adam clearly expected based on his experience with his father, this student invited Adam to offer an alternative explanation and answer to the latest crisis in the Middle East.

Adam was stunned. No one had ever asked him for his opinion. Adam's father had opinions and his father had taught him what he should believe about Israel. But Adam had never really thought through any issues for himself. Adam staggered off to class, for once his mouth shut.

For Adam, this was one of those existential, life-altering experiences one reads about in books or sees in the movies. But this was no movie. Adam didn't know what he believed in. He had always done just what his father had told him—or the exact opposite just to spite him. What were his views about Israeli politics and world events? Why did he follow a certain religion and not another? What did he want to do with his life? What did he really care about? Why was he even in college—how did he get there without even knowing what he wanted to study or do professionally?

Adam was both forlorn and exhilarated at the same time—forlorn because he had never before thought for himself about his life and values, exhilarated because here was his opportunity to do so. Adam didn't know what to do with himself.

For starters, Adam decided not to be so critical and outspoken, and he began to listen to others' views more closely. He decided to enroll in an Arab-Israeli conflict class in the political science department. And he realized that he could actually become educated and informed about a lot of political issues. "Wasn't that what he had heard his professor say," Adam thought, "that society desperately needs highly educated people who can analyze issues and make informed choices to help address the very complex and difficult challenges that face society?" Adam decided he could be one of those people.

He also dug out a high school graduation gift he thought he'd never use—a journal. Each day he began to write down what he believed in. He was amazed at all of the contradictions and inconsistencies in his views and arguments, but after a while, he began to find himself.

Adam was no longer merely a critic, a responder, with no views of his own. He found he was beginning to carve out his own meaning in life, his own set of values, his own direction, his own worldview. Sometimes his values overlapped with his dad's, and sometimes his views were quite different—but whatever the case, these were his own views. Adam was taking control of his life, and was he ever excited about his future! He started to get involved in campus organizations and politics, and by sophomore year, there he was, handing out flyers and exhorting the new college students to join his Israeli politics group.

55 Model a Sustainable Lifestyle

How are we going to survive as a planet? What steps are you going to take in your life to insure that we survive?

As much as the college years are a time to take control of your identity, your studies, and your relationships, it is also a time to take responsibility for your imprint on the planet. The frightening dangers to our very survival as a species are well-documented, and they will most certainly impact your lives and the lives of your children and grandchildren. You can no longer see yourself as just a consumer of the world's resources, but you also must re-imagine yourself as a caretaker of the planet and begin to model your values.

While the scope of the climate/environmental crisis is daunting, it still calls for change in small steps by each individual as well as national and global policy changes. So, start to think about what small steps you can take in your life at college to begin to have an impact. First, find out the size of your carbon footprint, and make a list of the ways that you can reduce that footprint. Look at your daily practice using lights, electricity, technology, cars, gas, air conditioning, and re-evaluate your usage. What are your recycling habits? What are your consumption habits?

Do you know where your food comes from? Do your food purchases support sustainable agriculture? What is the history of the salmon you are eating—is it wild salmon or farmed salmon (and farmed under what conditions)? What were the conditions of the farm and the cow and the workers and the meatpackers that led to the hamburger you are eating at this very moment? How much corn and corn byproducts are in the everyday foods you eat, why is that the case, and what does it mean for the health of the ecosystem and for your health? And how do the agribusiness processes and the policy decisions about how much meat and corn that is produced affect global climate? What is the likelihood of you and people around the world getting e-coli or other diseases from eating dinner tonight? Is your water safe to drink, and is it publicly or privately controlled?

What are the local initiatives in your college town to transition toward a more sustainable planet? Do you or the college cafeteria make decisions to purchase locally grown food? Is there public transportation to get around town? Do you walk or ride a bike? How do we manage the impact on our planet of the increasing globalization of our communities? As study abroad becomes more of an expectation for your college studies, are there other options to create international experiences, learning, and social networks apart from increasing the amount of air travel and resulting increase in jet fuel consumption? What policy initiatives can your campus and college town undertake to create a more sustainable present and future for all of us?

One of the goals of higher education is to develop an informed citizenry who will be active participants and leaders in a diverse democracy. You want to emerge from your college education as one of those active participants and leaders, whether at the local community level, in the Jewish community, or on regional, national, or global levels.

There are many different types of leaders and many different leadership opportunities. You should consider trying all of them to acquire experience and skills but also to see what fits you best. You have probably already had experience with the traditional model of leadership—a single head of a hierarchically arranged organization.

Living on your residence hall floor over the course of a year, you will be confronted with occasional roommate conflicts, arguments over loud music, inconsiderate and rude behavior, and perhaps even racial or religious insensitivities. Your floor will need a student who emerges as a leader, apart from the resident advisor, who will set the proper moral tone and create an environment in which people learn to talk through differences and disagreements.

In your classes, you can be an intellectual leader. You can do this by coming to class not only prepared (having completed the assignment) but also ready to ask probing questions and offer critical insights about the day's assignments. You can be a good listener and respond appropriately to other students' comments. You can attend faculty office hours. You can help organize study groups and support your fellow students who raise good issues or who come to you with questions.

In addition to hierarchical leadership, some people act as leaders through their ability to collaborate effectively with others. Working effectively in teams is a skill that most people require in all aspects of life, from the office to the community to home. Yet it is an exceedingly difficult skill and one that few people fully master. Finding opportunities to develop this skill through study groups, group papers, lab projects, research projects, and planning events for student organizations will serve you well and give you valuable experience.

Another kind of leadership is that of the boundary-crosser. Purposefully engage in meaningful ways with people and settings that are new to you. You will begin to gain the ability and readiness to cross boundaries not only without fear but with anticipation for the rich learning and growth that emerge from those interactions and associations. Those who can do this well will be highly effective in managing social relations in their social life and in the workplace.

At some colleges you will have an opportunity to demonstrate leadership by serving as a student facilitator of course discussions. Student facilitators lead discussions in service-learning courses, intergroup dialogues, university 101–type courses, and other situations. Taking on this role requires responsibility, organizational skills, good discussion and listening skills, and the ability to assert oneself and intervene when necessary.

Finally, in addition to all of these informal opportunities to develop leadership skills, many colleges offer classes, workshops, and retreats on leadership. In these activities, you will do readings, review case studies, and learn what makes good leaders in all of the different styles where leadership exists and is necessary. Students who participate in these activities tell me that they find them highly informative, empowering, and loads of fun.

One of the most novel innovations in higher education in recent years is what is called Alternative Spring Break. Instead of spending spring break flying to a beach town for revelry, thousands of students now use this time to work for a community in great need. It provides very useful service to the community and is an opportunity for deep learning for you.

The concept of Alternative Spring Break is important. The message is not just that one should look for an alternative to spring break. It also speaks to the voice of students saying that there is an alternative to always focusing on one's pleasure and self. Alternative Spring Break says it is important to care for and partner with others in need.

Recently, Alternative Weekends, a spinoff of Alternative Spring Break with the same orientation and values, have taken hold on many campuses. Like all volunteering and community service experiences, the learning takes place most effectively if you take time to prepare for the community with which you will work and if you take time to reflect on the experience. Be sure that you have these opportunities prior to and after the actual work at the site.

An important part of the attraction of this alternative is the close bond that develops among the participants. Students go in groups of ten to fifteen to Alternative Spring Break sites. They live, work, and socialize together. When a group really clicks, the relationships that grow and the learning that takes place are very powerful.

There are costs involved in Alternative Spring Break because students usually travel to cities and sites outside the region of their college. Thus, there are travel costs, food costs, and lodging costs, although lodging is usually arranged through the community site at local homes, community centers, or religious centers. As a group, students learn and do fund-raising for several months in advance in order to cover their expenses.

A wide range of sites can be selected. Students might work with the homeless, people with HIV/AIDS, children in failing schools, women's shelters, food kitchens, and so on. Students often work with ethnic and racial communities that are different from their own background. The college should be expected to do a thorough job of researching all these sites before arranging to send students.

No one will get famous for participating in these programs. You shouldn't expect any of the media attention, on campus and on national TV, that the traditional wild spring break parties get. Nevertheless, many students tell me that Alternative Spring Break and Alternative Weekends are transformative experiences, the highlight of their school year.

58 Learn to Collaborate with Your Peers

To succeed in your personal and professional life, you will need to have good skills in collaboration so that you can work effectively with people you like and befriend, those you don't know well or don't like, those who come from similar or different backgrounds from yours, and even those who hold different or competing values and personal styles than you.

High schools and colleges increasingly require students to work on joint projects, participate in study groups, and write papers together. The research on study groups clearly demonstrates that students, both those more and less advanced, learn more in groups than by exclusively studying alone.

If you're like many other students, I have no doubt that you're thinking that study groups and group projects don't always feel like they're very worthwhile. They can take more time, more social involvement, and more effort and can result in occasional struggles with one individual who does not come ready to do an equal share of the work. All of this reflects real life in the workplace and community, and these are important though sometimes unpleasant and painful skills to learn.

The key is that you want these collaborative projects to work well and efficiently, not badly. How do you do that? First, you have to come prepared. Second, you have to come with a readiness to learn and cooperate. Third, you must be prepared to be open to working and learning in a manner of equality with people who may have different learning and working styles, who may have different goals and ambitions, and who come from backgrounds different from yours.

One of the common problems in work projects is that people often reinforce societal stereotypes in their collaborations. In math study groups, for example, research has shown that men sometimes have lower expectations for the ability of women in the group and seek to dominate the discussion. Be sure to check your stereotypes and assumptions at the door—come with openness and high expectations for all participants.

It is important right from the start to determine how to share work responsibilities early in the project. If you're doing a group research project and paper, decide early on who will do which parts of the research—library research, data collection, interviews, and so on—and who will take responsibility for the writing. You may decide that each person will write a section of the paper, but then someone will need to rewrite so the paper has one voice. Another option is for a person who does less of the data collection to take responsibility for writing a draft of the paper and then have others revise and rewrite. It's always important to set strict timelines and check-in dates to be sure that all the required work is getting completed with high standards.

Study groups work the same way. Schedule meetings early and frequently. Decide who will facilitate each study group and who is responsible for presenting which aspects of the study preparation.

Sometimes everyone will need to be responsible for everything; other times you will want to share responsibilities. Decide early on the ground rules for continued participation and under what conditions a person may be asked to leave the group.

Collaboration skills come into play in almost everything you do. Developing these skills will serve you well in your personal and professional relationships, your learning, your growth and love of life, and your professional and career development.

6

Life on Campus
for Jewish Students

59   Get Along with Your Roommate

You'll be happiest if you start with positive yet modest expectations for your relationship with your roommate. You may hope for a perfect match, but you'll be more realistic if you anticipate that you'll have a reasonably respectful and civil relationship. Remember, you will spend eight to ten months in a small space, almost entirely filled with beds, desks, and dressers, together with a person (or persons) you've never met previously. The odds are on your side to have a perfectly good relationship, but don't count on perfect.

Students have lots of fantasies about their college roommates. You may have heard stories or watched TV shows where roommates are best friends and confidants. It does happen, it would be wonderful if it did, and it very well could. You may be thinking that you'll have similar tastes in room decoration, share values about neatness and cleanliness, and have good taste in friends. Your hope is that you'll share fears, celebrate successes, stay up late at night talking, and eat popcorn together watching favorite movies.

As hopeful but unlikely as this scenario is, it is just as unlikely that you and your roommate will be the very worst of matches. Your worst fears, that your roommate is a drug dealer, doesn't go to class, takes your things without asking, and is generally rude and disrespectful, are so unlikely that it's not worth giving much thought.

The actual experience of most students is a modestly positive one. You and your roommate are likely to get along just fine, although there may be some bumps in the road. You probably won't be each other's closest friends in the world, but you will share the experiences of one of your most memorable years. You will be able to negotiate most issues, such as differences about noise levels when one is sleeping, study time, and how to divide up the refrigerator. You may even end up liking and befriending some of your roommate's good friends.

It is critical that you approach your relationship with your roommate with respect, sensitivity, and civility. You have to learn to listen to his or her point of view, speak up for yourself and your views, speak openly and honestly, negotiate differences directly, and talk through any problems or disagreements.

Call your roommate during the summer before college to begin getting to know one another. Don't rush to decorate your room the day you move in without waiting to talk with your new roommate. Expect that he or she will have some different lifestyle habits and some different values from you. He may stay up late to study, while you go to bed early to wake up for eight o'clock classes. She may have five siblings and shared a room at home, while you have no siblings and have always had your own room. Your roommate will likely be different in some social identity, be it race, religion, class, ethnicity, or sexual orientation. Don't even think about the idea of rejecting a roommate because he or she comes from a different background (usually race). Be open to those differences, learn from them, and celebrate them.

It's not a good idea to room with your best friend from high school. Yes, it can work in some cases, but more often best friends stay best friends when they don't live together.

Be the wonderful, kind, agreeable person you are, and your roommate is likely to respond in kind.

60　Enjoy Life in the Residence Hall

For students living on campus, much of your first year of college will take place in your new home, the college residence hall. You should plan to make the most of the experience.

You will want, of course, to make friends in your residence hall. Hopefully, you and other students on your floor and elsewhere in the hall will go to meals together, go to social events, and walk to class together in the morning. Enjoy this rare opportunity to have so many friends living together under one roof.

You need to be on good behavior in the residence hall. You need to be respectful of others and work toward building a healthy and strong community on your floor and in your building. You will be sharing a bathroom with many others, so clean up after yourself (and be sure to thank the housekeeping person who does the thorough cleanup on your floor every day). In your room, put your trash and recycling in the proper bins. When you play music, keep the sound within the confines of your own room. Be sensitive to the different musical tastes of people on your floor.

Your resident advisor (RA) is a person you will want to meet on move-in day. The RA is an upper-class student who lives on your floor and whose job it is to be there for you whenever you need help. See the RA if you need to find out tips about campus life, if you have problems with a roommate or someone on the floor and have difficulty resolving the issue among yourselves, or if you have questions about how to access college resources.

Living in a residence hall is one of the best opportunities you will ever have to expand your social boundaries. Hopefully, you will have a chance to meet people from many different social identity groups and all parts of the country and world. Be sure to take advantage of this opportunity. Once you live outside of the residence halls, you won't have this opportunity again. In fact, it is frequently observed that the two institutions/locations where there is the greatest opportunity to interrupt the pervasive social segregation across race and religion in the U.S. are the military and the college residence hall during the first year of college.

Students almost universally complain about food in the residence hall. It's a tradition. The truth, though, is that residence hall food these days is plentiful, varied, and quite tasty. At most colleges, you will have your choice of entrees, salad bar, breakfast foods, soft drinks, and desserts at every meal, and all prepared for you. No cooking, no dishwashing. Your biggest challenge will not be that you can't find food to eat but that you will have to limit yourself. It would get monotonous to eat every meal every day even at your favorite restaurant. So, go ahead and complain about dorm food if you must, but tell the dining hall staff the truth—the food's pretty great, and you really appreciate the fact that they're cooking and you're not. And make your parent(s) happy by saying that you miss home cooking. They'll feel good knowing that you have not forgotten them.

Finally, college residence halls work very hard to be educational centers not just dormitories, hostels, or apartments. Take advantage of the residential colleges, living-learning programs, educational activities, faculty speakers, and volunteer activities that are organized through the residence hall. Remember to learn from every experience in college, both curricular and cocurricular.

61 Join Campus Organizations and Participate in Campus Activities

Are you wondering what you'll be doing each day at college with all the free time you have? Are you worried about being bored, that nothing will interest you, that you'll just be sitting in your room wasting away the hours? Then think again.

Outside of studying, which no doubt will take more of your time than you anticipate, there will be more events to attend and activities to participate in than you could ever imagine. Do you even want to try to count the number of student organizations on your campus? For many campuses, guess a number in the many hundreds. How about the number of activities that will be available to you during your first year of college? For that answer, guess the number of days of the academic year, then multiply by the many tens of activities that take place each day.

One of the biggest problems in getting involved is figuring out how to make sense of all that's going on. How do you access the rich resources of your campus? Online social networks and the campus newspaper are always good resources to find lists of events, as is the campus information center, often located in the student union. The student union and other campus buildings, including your residence hall, will have bulletin boards covered with posters and announcements of activities. Get in the habit of reading those boards. You should, of course, go online and identify a few key campus websites that are regularly updated and check them frequently. Your living-learning community is a very good pathway to getting involved in campuswide organizations. Friends, professors, and other word-of-mouth sources are probably your best resources—keep talking and listening.

Many campuses have big fairs near the start of school to introduce you to all the organizations on campus. Be sure to put your name and email address on the sign-up lists and social network fan pages for any that seem safe and even of moderate interest. Don't be shy about getting on these contact lists. They will allow you to be aware of organizational meetings and of opportunities to get involved. Many campus organizations also have open houses or mass meetings to recruit and welcome new students. Of course, you don't need to wait for organizations to contact you. Don't hesitate to ask online or to email or call any organization you're even vaguely interested in to find out when they are meeting. Be sure to go to those first meetings to check out the people, the mood, and the activities and opportunities that exist for new members and to see whether the group is a good fit for you.

There are a dizzying array of activities to choose from and get involved in on campus. Don't be overwhelmed by the choices. Try out new activities that you think you'll like and try entirely new possibilities with the expectation that some will appeal to you and others won't. Take your level of involvement one day at a time. Don't forget to become a fan of your classmates who are involved in other activities—team sports, theatrical or musical performances, or the like. Manage your time, stay active, explore the new and the old, enrich and expand your world, and have a terrific college experience.

JOEL COHEN—*"Vote for Me! Your Next President of the United States!"*

Don't underestimate Joel Cohen. Joel isn't a cocky guy, but he is a man on a mission. He has his mind set. Joel Cohen is on the road to becoming the first Jewish president of the United States!

Joel grew up in a wealthy and largely white and Jewish suburb of Chicago. He is a natural charmer. Handsome, smart, popular, athletic, and very ambitious—that is Joel Cohen in a nutshell. He was president of his high school, star receiver on his team's state championship football team, and winner of all kinds of awards and prizes. Joel excelled in history and English, completed several AP courses, and received lots of offers for college admissions. Joel has lots of friends, both male and female.

When Joel arrived at college, he immediately looked for leadership opportunities. Joel wasn't really shocked, but he couldn't help but notice that lots of other students on campus had been leaders at their high schools and also had high expectations for becoming campus leaders. The college had lots of bright, assertive, popular students—just like him.

But Joel was not deterred. Actually, he thrived on the success of others and thought it was great to be among such a talented group of students. Joel got situated in his classes, looked around campus a bit to see what opportunities existed, and then jumped in.

Academically, Joel enrolled in an undergraduate research program in political polling, in which he got to work on a project with a leading national pollster. His primary goal, of course, was to get to know a faculty member on a personal basis. He also took a first-year seminar in history, a small class of fifteen students, where he came to know his professor and fellow students individually.

Politically, the opportunities were enormous. Joel started out by running for office in his residence hall and was elected president of the Hall Council. That was a good way to make linkages across campus with other student leaders, but it also mostly limited him to first- and second-year students.

As Joel thought about other options, he considered writing for the student newspaper as he had in high school. That would have been lots of fun, but it was also a major time commitment, so he held off on that option. He attended a few meetings of the campus chapter of a national political party, but he was turned off by some of the seniors who were the current officers.

Finally, Joel decided he would run for campuswide student government office in the spring term election in order to serve in his sophomore year. Student politics, he found, were much more cutthroat in college than they had been in high school, with lots of dirty tricks and nasty personal game playing. Some students didn't like that Joel was Jewish, and most just didn't like his ambition and success. After all, they had goals very similar to Joel's—becoming the top student leaders on campus. Joel didn't care much for that kind of nastiness, but he was determined to go after his goal and knew it was important to be known on campus. His friends told him he looked more and more stressed out, but Joel knew that would necessarily come with the territory of political office.

Happily, Joel was elected in a close race to be one of his school's representatives to the campuswide student government. This was all part of his plan. In this, his first year, he had been elected to two different campus offices. Joel was starting to be known as one of the young campus leaders, and he was gaining influence and status. College had started very successfully.

What lay ahead for Joel? He hoped to run for campus president in the next academic year and was looking for internships in Washington, DC, with his congressman this summer and with his senator the next summer. He would major in political science and go to law school, and his future seemed as bright as possible—Joel was on his way to becoming the first Jewish president of the United States.

62 Go to Lectures, Museums, Workshops, Talks, and Concerts

If you keep in mind the notion of college as a scholarly community, you will quickly realize that your community is an environment filled with the riches of intellectual, cultural, and social learning. You should take full advantage of all of these aspects of learning in the community.

Every college campus has numerous guest speakers and lectures. People who are world famous as well as those who are brilliant and wonderful but less well known will be visiting your college every year for talks in academic departments and in policy meetings with administrators and faculty. Authors, poets, and artists give wonderful readings and performances.

Most of these visitors love to spend time with students and make themselves available to give talks, have dinner with students, or visit classrooms. Don't miss out on these scholars, political figures, and artists. They will enrich your life and expand your scholarly community.

Student groups also sponsor guest speakers who are well-known public, media, or governmental leaders. This is a great opportunity to see firsthand people you've seen, read, and heard about in the news, in books, or on TV. Seeing them in person will give you a whole new perspective on who they are and what they represent. You will be drawn to some, repulsed by others, and entertained by still others.

Similarly, all kinds of great theater and musical concerts from around the world will be available to you in college, usually at discounted student rates. If you attend college in an urban area, you may find that you have a much wider variety of these enrichment experiences to choose from, but you'll have to travel off campus to attend. It's good to take advantage of activities off campus as much as you can. If you're on a campus that is not in an urban area, then it's more likely that the performances will come to you, but probably there will be fewer choices. In either case, your response should be the same—make a point of attending.

Don't forget all the museums you can visit. Your college or your city will have any number of art and natural science museums to explore. Use these visits as an opportunity to build on what you've learned in your art history, archaeology, and science classes.

The campus will also have numerous different racial, ethnic, religious, and cultural groups. Many of these groups hold special concerts and celebrations that are open to the entire campus. These performances can be spectacular, invigorating, and inspiring for both participating college peers and audience members. Such events are not to be missed.

Attending these lectures, concerts, museums, and performances will broaden your horizons immeasurably. You should develop these habits for your entire life. The truth of the matter is, however, that now is the time to take full advantage of these opportunities because in college you are likely to have more unstructured time, fewer responsibilities for children and parents, and much more deeply discounted tickets than you will have after you leave college.

63 Stay Connected and Involved in Campus Life as a Commuter Student

If you commute to campus, there are lots of reasons why it's more difficult for you to be actively involved in campus life, but none of those reasons are good enough to keep you away. You just have to make up your mind that you're going to be actively involved and then follow through on that commitment. It's important for your education, for your connections with faculty and fellow students, and for your personal and social development. It will make a difference in the likelihood of your academic success.

One of the keys to both college satisfaction and success is the degree to which you feel connected or linked to the institution. Feeling connected through academics is the best way to do this, but it's also critical to make these connections through campus-life activities.

A good first way to make campus more than a disparate series of classes and exams is to find a physical space that is your home on campus. It's good to have a sense of place for anything that's important to you. The best way to accomplish this as a commuter student, though it will take some time, is for you to be so involved in a campus organization that you get to use the offices of the organization as a place where you can leave your things, study, and be with people. A second choice is to find a locker or a room on campus where you can safely leave your belongings and where you can return each day you come to campus. In addition to this locker or room, find a couple other locations that you can claim as home. One might be at a friend's campus apartment or a particularly good study space in one of the libraries or coffee shops, or you might want to find a favorite lounge chair or table in the student union near some good eateries.

Some learning communities on commuter campuses have talked about creating special physical spaces for commuter students. The goal of doing so would be to bring the commuter students together into a more cohesive community on campus. Find out if your learning community or college has set aside any space for you, as a commuter student, to create a place for yourself.

As a commuter student, your time is much less flexible than the college campus often expects. Therefore, it is your responsibility to carefully structure your schedule and manage your time. With regard to participating in campus organizations and attending campus events, you will need to be more attentive to scheduling conflicts and time demands than other students. You may want to try to take late classes on certain days so you can also attend events or meetings in the evening while keeping other days free for work and family. As long as you have a secure place to leave your belongings, you will be much more flexible to coordinate your campus days than if you have to carry everything with you each time you come to campus. Ask the organizations you want to participate in to be sensitive to your constraints and to try to work with your schedule, just as you are trying to adapt to theirs. Do your utmost to make these arrangements work.

64 Find Your Jewish Community

As part of the wealth of opportunities to make friends, join organizations, and get involved in campus life, you will want to find your place in the Jewish community. There you will have the opportunity to meet friends who share a common background, holidays, experiences, values, cultural ways, and histories.

It's a misnomer, of course, to speak of "a" Jewish community as if it's a monolithic community or a single organization. Similarly, it's also a mistake to imagine that the people you will meet in the Jewish community will not have just as many differences in experience, background, values, and religious practice as shared common ground. However, I mention this as a good thing for you and the Jewish community. You should anticipate the likelihood of becoming part of many Jewish communities and making friends with many different sets of Jewish peers. If you happen to meet some Jewish students whom you don't like or happen to hear about a Jewish organization you want no part of, don't worry. There will be other Jewish students that you do like, and there will be another organization that seems much better suited to your interests.

Some students come to college with an intact Jewish community from Jewish youth groups or temple at home, from Jewish summer camp, or from a gap year in Israel together. These communities are wonderful foundations from which to build upon your college Jewish community. Because you want to move on beyond your high school experiences, however, you will want to be sure to broaden, widen, and deepen your circles with new Jewish peers, with Jews from different backgrounds and experiences, and with interests that challenge you in ways that are constructive and help you learn and grow.

If you are religiously observant, you will meet Jewish students at the first Shabbat service and at a kosher dinner if your campus offers such a service. You may not be a regular schul-goer, but still one who wants to meet other Jews at a Friday night dinner at Hillel or Chabad House. Interested in studying about Jewish topics? You will meet other Jewish students at Judaic studies and Hebrew language classes at your university, and those classes will often be smaller than most others. Interested in Israel? There will be organizations aligned with more conservative and more liberal political positions that will look for you to get involved. Interested in campus politics, theater, environmental groups, the school newspaper, or community service? You will find other Jewish students involved in these activities. Interested in socializing and living with other Jewish students? Then you may want to rush a Jewish fraternity or sorority. Or, if you are gay, you will want to seek out the campus Jewish LGBT group that may hold its meetings at the Hillel House.

You may also want to hang out with a much more diverse group of students than just other Jews. Guess what? You'll also find other Jewish students in these diverse groups. The point is that there are all kinds of Jews with all kinds of interests. It would do you well to meet the diversity of the Jewish student communities on campus, and not just fall back exclusively on the same religious, cultural, Israel-focused group of Jews that you either loved or avoided in high school.

Hillel is the best known destination for Jewish life on the college campus. Most Hillels have numerous student organizations that support almost any Jewish interest whether it be religious, cultural, social, or educational. There is always a very devoted group of students for whom Hillel becomes their Jewish and campus home. At the same time, Hillel isn't a good fit for every Jewish student. Not a problem. Just start your own organization at Hillel or look for another way to get involved Jewishly there.

Chabad has a rabbi and his family on many Jewish campuses and a smaller number of students are overjoyed at the personal and welcoming invitation the rabbi extends to students to join his family for Shabbat dinner. For these students, Chabad's outreach can seem more genuine, personal, and less bureaucratic than the Jewish organizational life they have previously experienced. And, yet, for many other Jewish students, the approach of Chabad and its rabbi is something they want no part of.

In some urban areas, there are welcoming community synagogues/ temples and community centers where you can find religious, cultural, and social homes. There are other Jewish outreach organizations on campus that have national affiliations to recruit students for a variety of purposes, whether to support political perspectives about Israel or become more religiously observant (some cover all student expenses to attend national conferences or even pay students to study Jewish texts). Many students look into these organizations as well and can become very active. Other students get turned off by their politics, by the leaders, or by their religious "agendas." I have also heard from students who were deeply offended by some organizations that didn't consider them to be Jewish because of an interfaith marriage or a conversion they didn't recognize—so they moved on and found an alternative place to form their Jewish community.

Jewish life is often structured by its organizations, of which there are a multitude. However, Jewish community can grow in more informal ways rather than just through organizations, and many young Jews have intentionally sought and found Jewish community outside formal Jewish organizations. Hanging out at the coffee shop with Jewish friends, celebrating Friday night Shabbat dinner with a few friends at your apartment, going to a movie with other Jews, or starting up a project with a small group without all the bureaucratic trappings of Jewish organizations is how some Jewish students find their Jewish community.

There are so many opportunities to develop your Jewish community(ies) at college. Find Jewish friends and community that share commonalities with you. At the same time, go out and meet the diversity of the Jewish community, learn about your differences, and make them part of your Jewish communities, too. Try out Hillel and other Jewish organizations and Jewish student groups and see if they will be a community for you. And discover the Jewish communities that emerge organically around you, with friends who share common purpose and commitment in the world.

65 Navigate and Learn from Your Experience as a Religious Minority on Campus

The fact is that for the last fifty-plus years higher education in the United States has served Jews as one of the best examples of the American ideals of freedom and opportunity. Despite being such a small minority in this country, Jews today are fully represented in every sector of our universities, from students to faculty to administrators and trustees. You will find Jews who are presidents of the entire campus student body, powerful deans of schools and colleges, and presidents of universities. You will almost certainly take courses with several Jewish faculty just by randomly selecting classes without attention to their identity. Higher education, indeed, is a welcoming home for the new Jewish student.

Still, most Jewish students, like most Americans, live in neighborhoods and attend K–12 schools that are homogeneous in terms of religion, race, and class. If you are like most Jewish students, then, this means that you will have spent a majority of your time growing up with other Jews, a majority of whom are also white and middle/upper class.

Most Jewish students, therefore, will find themselves in an unfamiliar situation when they attend college, albeit with a few notable exceptions like Brandeis U. or Yeshiva U., and represent a minority presence amidst a majority Christian student body. Although the experience of being a minority has been a constant for Jews throughout history, for young Jews in the U.S. who have grown up among other Jews, this may come as quite a surprise.

One of the privileges of being in the majority is that most times one does not have to be aware of one's social identity and can self-identify and make attributions as an individual. For instance, many of my white students, when asked to think about race, will tell me that race has to do with people of color, not themselves. My male students, similarly, have infrequently thought about gender issues, and will tell me that gender is a topic for women, not men. Wealthier students often think that class issues are about the lower economic classes, not about themselves. On the other hand, in each of these examples, people of color, women and less wealthy students, unlike their counterparts, are acutely aware of the behaviors and attitudes that are presented as the norms of society that advantage the majority, privileged groups.

Jewish students may thus be surprised when they arrive at college to find that their experiences, their language, their holidays, their foods, and their religion are not the norm on campus. It's likely you will become increasingly aware of just how different some of your experiences and practices are from your peers who are Christian, Muslim, Hindu, Buddhist, etc. One early shock may be that no one but other Jewish students has any idea or interest in the fact that the Jewish High Holy Days are arriving in September and it will require you to make difficult choices about attending class or other events in the first weeks of school. Your roommate may ask you to translate some of your funny words like Shabbat or Challah, question your interest in kosher deli or gefilte fish, or wonder why you seem so obsessed with news about Israeli politics. An infrequent, but still not uncommon, jolt may come from a roommate or classmate who has never before met a Jewish person.

Less amusing will be the loss of some of your individuality. Some of your peers will ascribe stereotypes, both positive and negative, to you, that may have little if anything to do with your individual personality and values. At the very moment you are setting forth your own independent adult identity, others will be making assumptions that you are a bright, high achieving business student, or that you are very brash and aggressive, or that you are a "Jewish American Prince or Princess." When there is an incident on campus involving a Jewish fraternity or a Jewish student running for student government president, your non-Jewish friends may offer explanations for the incident based on the Jewish identity of those involved rather than any factual information about the individuals or the incidents.

You may also be surprised when your peers ask you why you are not going to church on Sunday or if you want to join them for a Bible study group and the text is not the Torah but the New Testament. Those odd comments exploring your religious background when you rush a sorority may seem perplexing at the moment until you later realize that the membership is predominantly Christian.

It may help you understand your situation to rethink how you have reacted in similar situations but ones in which you were the majority group. It probably won't be hard to recall stereotypes made by Jewish friends about people of color back at your high school lunch table, or to remember your rushing a Jewish sorority and the questions about religious background you heard asked of non-Jews by the other Jewish sorority girls. You may realize, too, that you know virtually nothing about the Christian religion and other religions and religious practices, just like you were so surprised that non-Jewish students knew so little about Judaism.

When it comes to discussion of Israeli-Palestinian issues on campus, you may be surprised to see a much more vigorous and heated debate than you ever witnessed at your schul or Jewish community center. You may hear things you agree or disagree with, and that sometimes offend you, but you will be well-served to educate yourself and become better informed, listen to various viewpoints, and to engage in these important discussions. College campuses are institutions where free speech and the exchange of ideas and viewpoints are meant to flourish, so learn from the discussions and join in with your informed opinion.

You may also be surprised to be confronted by ignorance, insensitivity, and blatant anti-Semitism during your college years. At one time or another over your four years, you may find yourself reading ugly anti-Semitic rants on bathroom walls, hear fellow students making jokes about Jews, or discover that some Jews on campus have been confronted by individuals shouting hateful epithets. Some students on campus may try to convert you to Christianity. You may even come across a professor or administrator whose attitude and approach toward Jews seems suspect. Don't be afraid to stand up for yourself as a Jew and learn how to do so effectively, and with pride.

The fact is that most college campuses are very tolerant, respectful, and open communities. Most of the questions that come your way will come out of respect and a sincere desire to learn from you, even if sometimes you are taken aback. You can further your awareness and that of your peers by engaging in substantive, open discussions with them and even joining an interfaith dialogue. Be aware and learn from how you react to those in privileged majority roles to better understand your own behavior and attitudes in your privileged social identities, and explore how you might make the kinds of changes that you appreciate from your friends of other religious backgrounds. Finally, you should use the opportunity of being a religious minority at college to learn to live productively in a diverse, pluralistic society, become skilled as a boundary-crosser, and engage with peers from different backgrounds even as you strengthen your own Jewish identity.

MICHAEL WEINGARTEN—*"I'm Older but Newer: After the Gap Year in Israel."*

Michael Weingarten had a great year in Israel following his high school graduation. He was steeped in good friendships, Jewish life, Israeli culture, Torah study and Jewish learning, and falafel and hummus. He felt he had grown a lot in the last year and was very pleased with his decision to live in Israel and wait a year to go to college back home in the States.

Michael had chosen a university with a relatively large Jewish population. But in deciding not to attend Brandeis or yeshiva, he knew it was going to be a culture shock returning to a society that wasn't predominantly Jewish. Would he find a good Jewish community? Could he continue his Jewish studies? Would he be isolated wearing his kippah in public? Could he find kosher food and a good falafel sandwich?

Michael was happily surprised to find that he fit right in at college. The Jewish community was lively, diverse, and full of ruach. There were many options for both religiously observant and less observant students. Kosher food was not a big problem. There was a lot of good energy around Israel issues. He loved the breadth of Judaic Studies courses. Clearly, college was not his gap year in Israel, but he was doing fine Jewishly.

Personally and socially, however, it was something of a transition for Michael. While he was, in fact, a first-year student, he was a year older. He wasn't like all the other students who were coming to school right out of college, but he was placed in all of their orientation sessions and welcome activities. The worries he had, and he was anxious, were different from the worries of the first-year students. He wasn't full of the typical first-year excitement about the sudden independence, the chance to drink and act out, or the opportunity to live in a dorm with other eighteen year olds. In fact, he didn't quite feel like he fit in with those students, and he didn't really want to fit in. He was older and had already had his year of growing up away from home.

Academically, Michael was very interested in taking the upper level courses being offered like his friends who were sophomores, but he was still required to complete the introductory prerequisite courses. He felt more worldly and wiser than his first-year peers in these classes, but in many ways they were more accustomed to the academic rigor and routine of tests and papers than he was. He found he was a bit rusty and realized it would take a little time for him to get up to speed.

In his first sociology class, he wrote his first paper in a manner that his teachers in Israel would have loved. He referenced texts from the Bible and Rabbinical scholars. He based his arguments on Jewish law. He proudly turned in his paper and anxiously awaited his professor's comments and grade.

When the papers were returned to students in class, Michael was shocked to read the comments. Instead of the expected A grade, the professor asked Michael to come see him at office hours because his paper "was not acceptable." Michael had never written a paper that was not acceptable, and he had never received a grade lower than a B.

Michael nervously awaited the day of his professor's office hours. "Michael," the professor said, "this is a sociology class. You need to think as a sociologist, as a social scientist, in this class. You've written a paper that your rabbi might find very worthwhile, but it's not sociology." Michael wasn't sure whether to be defensive—"was this professor against me because I used Jewish references"—or to be very grateful that this professor was taking the time to introduce him to college learning. "Michael," the professor continued, "if your Bible teacher in Israel had assigned you a paper to give a religious interpretation of Bible text, and you turned in a sociological analysis, he would probably find it interesting but not likely acceptable for his class. I'm asking you to think as a social scientist and you need to do that in this course. It's great that you can think in ways that the yeshiva promotes, but it is also essential that you learn how to bring social scientific analysis to this subject matter if you want to think like a social scientist and do well in this college."

"Michael, if you're interested, I'd like you to re-write your paper and give this a try, and I will ignore the grade from your first effort. I think it will help you be a successful college student."

Michael "got" it. There was a methodology of study at his yeshiva in Israel, and a methodology of study at his secular university in the U.S. These methodologies weren't mutually exclusive and Michael knew he would be all the better and wiser to be successful in both modes of learning. Michael re-wrote his paper and received a B+ from his professor.

As time went on that fall semester, Michael began to make new, good friends in the Jewish community on campus and got involved in lots of college clubs and activities where he met other Jews and non-Jews alike. He realized he had already learned some important lessons at college, and he was now ready to be as successfully academically at college as he felt he was Jewishly and socially.

Some of the most important lessons you will learn in college will take place outside the classroom.

You can learn from every individual you encounter and every activity you participate in, no matter where or when those interactions take place, as long as you make a point of reflecting on those encounters and experiences. College is an environment of intentional learning, and you should begin to think of yourself as an intentional learner. Maximize your opportunities for learning as deeply and as broadly as possible from all your college-related experiences.

You should consider a variety of categories of learning outside the classroom. Consider first what may seem to be the easiest and most natural, hanging out with friends. At college, you have a chance to broaden your scope of friends. If you step outside your room, you are likely to meet individuals who come from a much wider variety of racial, ethnic, religious, class, and sexual orientation backgrounds than you have previously been exposed to or been friendly with. Get to know these people. Make friends with them. In time, open up yourself to them about your background and learn about theirs.

Second, get involved. Play on sports teams. Join a Jewish organization, the drama club, the chemistry club, the student newspaper, or your residence hall council. Volunteer for a community service project, take on an internship, find a job. All of these activities will give you insight into how organizations and people within organizations work in different sectors of society. Are the organizations highly structured or unstructured, hierarchical or authority sharing? Do people involved work competitively or collaboratively, do they do things together outside of work, or does everyone go their own way immediately after a meeting or the job is done?

Third, attend all sorts of campus events, including those that are social, educational, and cultural. Go to a football or hockey game.

Attend the opera, a chamber orchestra concert, a comedian's performance, a musical production, or a Shabbat service. Go to a panel discussion about global warming or Arab-Israeli issues, a presentation on interfaith or race relations, a talk about the human genome, a workshop on getting along with your roommate, or a documentary about endangered species. Go by yourself, with a friend, or with a large group from your residence hall. You will be exposed to a wide range of life from many different vantage points. Enjoy yourself, and learn about the world around you.

Finally, get involved in campus and community organizations to learn leadership skills. Run for an office in student government. Take a position in a departmental club. Train to become a student facilitator for an intergroup dialogue class. Be a site leader one day a week for the local food kitchen. Let a faculty member or dean know that you'd like to be a student representative on a faculty committee. Attend leadership workshops or retreats. You will learn about different kinds of leadership, where your strengths lie, and how you like to participate in organizations.

College is an all-day, every-day learning experience, and you should take advantage of the immense learning opportunities available both inside and outside of the classroom.

67 Consider Whether Fraternities and Sororities Are for You

Your decision as to whether or not to join a fraternity or sorority can have a big impact on how you experience college.

The myths and stereotypes of fraternities and sororities, both good and bad, are legendary and extreme. Jewish fraternities, for better or worse, have in recent years represented the full spectrum of behavior of the wider cohort. The truth is that there are many different types of fraternities and sororities on every college campus, some resembling the best and some the very worst of the stereotypes, with many falling closer to the middle. In most cases, however, they do represent a significant investment of time, money, and emotional commitment. Therefore, you should make this choice carefully and deliberately.

Fraternities and sororities have a number of different organizational foci. Find out what types of organizations exist on your campus and what percentage of students participate.

The majority are social organizations, with an emphasis on group bonding, social cohesion, and social activities to bring the membership together. There are also a smaller number that have service as their primary focus, providing educational support or tutoring to students on campus and sometimes in the community. An even smaller number come together for religious fellowship.

Most fraternities and sororities belong to the national umbrella groups, the Interfraternity Conference or Panhellenic Conference. While these organizations are open to all students, individual houses are predominantly and sometimes exclusively white and heterosexual, and many tend to be religiously homogeneous, such as many of the Jewish fraternities and sororities. Similarly, the Black Greek Association includes fraternities and sororities that tend to be predominantly or exclusively Black. In recent years, there have emerged a growing number of independent fraternities and sororities that are Latino, Asian American, gay/lesbian, or intentionally multiethnic.

The great appeal of these organizations, of course, is the strong friendships and professional networks that evolve over time, in some cases lasting for a lifetime. However, those friendships grow, in part, because of the intensity of the group activities coupled with the very demanding time commitments required of new pledges and members.

Those nonacademic time commitments, particularly during the first semester of college, create critical academic problems for a certain number of students each year.

In response to the downsides of the time commitment and the staging of rush activities right when students enter college, a growing number of fraternities and sororities are moving rush to the second semester or second year of college, as is the practice of the Black Greek Association. Timing is one of the things you should consider when deciding whether and when to rush a fraternity or sorority.

The continuing homogeneity of fraternities and sororities is another important consideration. On many campuses, students in fraternities and sororities, particularly white students on predominantly white campuses, are among the most isolated on campus in terms of social diversity. This can also be the case for Jewish students in predominantly or exclusively Jewish fraternities and sororities. Some in the Jewish community view this Jewish homogeneity as a major asset because it holds the possibility for Jewish college students to build strong Jewish communities, networks, and Jewish-Jewish romantic relationships.

Diversity is an important part of your education and growth in college, so you should consider how well you will be able to address that value of college if you join a fraternity or sorority that is both homogeneous and very demanding of your time and attention. This is another opportunity to invoke the "both/and" principle. How can you most effectively balance both your commitment and ties to Jewish friends and the Jewish community while at the same time fully embrace and participate in the rich diversity of a pluralistic college community, society, and global community?

The final consideration is the behavior of the overall Greek system on your campus and the student members who are in the individual fraternities or sororities you would consider rushing. Fit is everything here. To what extent does the culture of the sorority or fraternity you wish to rush match your values in terms of academic achievement, social relationships, alcohol use, Jewish identity, diversity, and respect for self and others. It's a good time to examine what you hope to gain from your college education and to consider to what extent fraternity/sorority life will enhance or detract from your goals.

Don't rush your decision about rush. Make a careful, thoughtful choice that will be best for you.

7

Chicken Soup: Health and Safety for the Body and Mind

68 Learn to Enjoy Yourself, Learning, and the College Experience

Your life will be much more fulfilling and satisfying if you learn to enjoy who you are and what you do.

You have four or more years of college ahead of you, an intensive learning focus throughout college, and, in the years beyond, a lifetime of being with yourself. All of that will be a lot more pleasant if you can find the secret of happiness at college, in your learning, and with yourself.

You need to be clear that happiness is not always a ball of laughter. Happiness is not the same as partying. It is important that you be clear about what is meaningful and fulfilling in your life. Money alone or A grades by themselves will not necessarily bring you happiness or enjoyment.

In college, you should focus on both the outcome and the process. One outcome is that you will obtain a degree at the end. A second outcome is that you will be a well-educated person. A third outcome is that you will be prepared to be an active and engaged participant in your community in a diverse democracy. A fourth outcome is that you have become an independent adult. You should feel good if you're making progress toward those goals.

It's equally important, however, that you learn to enjoy the process of getting to those outcomes. Much of the college experience centers on learning. If you focus only on your grades and not on what you are learning, you may achieve your ultimate goal but be a very unhappy person along the way. If you find classes boring and studying drudgery, you're in trouble. You want to develop a love of learning. You want to look forward to the intellectual energy of a class discussion with faculty and peers; the exposure to new ideas, perspectives, and discoveries in course readings and assignments; and the intrinsic intellectual thrill every time you gain a new insight.

You can worry too much about tests so that you are miserable even when you do well. You can stress constantly about your grade point average so that you are never satisfied or fulfilled, even with perfection. You can be so obsessed with the outcome of graduating from college that you never enjoy the beauty of attending college.

The same holds true for enjoying yourself. You need to learn to live comfortably and amicably with yourself. You need to find pleasure and satisfaction in your thoughts, values, actions, and outlook. You need to feel good about yourself, about how you are continuing to develop and grow, and about your abilities to change those areas you want to improve.

You may set goals for yourself, but if you don't enjoy the path to achieving the goals, the successful outcome may not bring you the satisfaction you desire. In college, you want to learn about yourself so you can be a person you like and admire. You want to learn how to enjoy the process of learning because so much of your time and energy will be spent learning. You want to be happy about earning your college degree, but you also want to enjoy the experience of getting your college education.

69 Live a Well-Rounded Life

You want to grow and develop as a whole person in college. In order to do this, you need to find ways to be a well-rounded person who takes advantage of the wide range of opportunities available in college.

Academics are at the center of a college education. Achieving academic success, in terms of mastery of academic content, skills, and processes, is a critical goal. Developing as an adult and learning how you can best make a difference in the world as an educated individual is a necessity. Learning skills in problem solving, building relationships, and managing conflicts are essential.

To accomplish all of these important goals in college, you will need to find balance in your life. You want to begin modeling a healthy, balanced lifestyle that you can sustain throughout your life.

Your challenge during college is to succeed academically but at the same time to allow yourself to grow and blossom in many aspects of your life. To do this, you will need to learn to effectively manage your time and make difficult choices.

You will find you have to spend more time studying in college than in high school. You will have so much unstructured time that you will find yourself staying up late but wondering where all the hours of the day went. You will be thrilled with all the wonderful opportunities to learn and participate outside the classroom, but in order to keep your head in the books, you'll have to learn to sometimes say no to those activities and to good friends. And, for some students, the opposite will be the case. You'll have to learn to say yes to go out, to be with friends and do things outside of the classroom, and to get your head out of the books.

Some students talk about a lifestyle whereby they "study hard and party hard." That works for some, but I'm not sure that's the best approach either. I think it can lead to a binge mentality that leads to extremes, like workaholic and alcoholic tendencies. I advocate lightening up a bit on yourself and developing a lifestyle that you can sustain over your lifetime.

Live a balanced and well-rounded life. Learn to enjoy your studies, enjoy learning, enjoy your time with friends, and love life itself.

70 Take Care of Your Soul

As much as your mind and your physical body need your care, attention, and stimulation, so does your inner soul. Feed and nurture it, and you will be that much stronger and more grounded to face each day.

Beyond any material goals or even academic achievements, what is important to you in life? What are your values? When you get down to the essentials in your life, what matters most? What keeps you going each day? What is your purpose in life?

You will know if you are having academic troubles in your classes because your professor will speak to you or you will find yourself getting grades that are below your expectations or are simply not passing. Your mind will let you know whether you are stimulated by your teachers and by the related intellectual content of the courses. Your body will tell you if you are not feeling well or if you have sustained an injury.

It's just as important to have some mechanisms to keep track of whether your soul is healthy or aching. Do people speak well of you, the person, not just of your accomplishments or the clothes you wear? Do your friends like you because of your generous spirit, or do they like you because you own a fancy car or have a new TV in your room? Do you like yourself because of your good looks, because of awards you have received, or because you like what you stand for in the world?

Do you feel good about who you are? Do you not only like the personality you present to others but also like the person inside whom you know better than anyone else? Can you not only live with yourself but also appreciate and respect who you are?

You may want to determine what things nurture your soul. It might be a good friendship. It might be good family relationships. You could be heartened by the story of someone's life that you read about in a book or watch in a movie. Perhaps you feel good after doing something good for another person, for your community, or for an animal or for the environment. You might need to learn something new and inspiring, appreciate a work of art or music, or gain insight into something you never understood before. Your soul might be nurtured by your connection with Judaism, by praying, or by appreciating the bounty of the earth when you eat some fresh fruit and vegetables. You might get this feeling from a deeply moving conversation with a friend, a teacher, a parent, or grandparent or from the joy of holding a newborn baby.

Being healthy has many dimensions. Be sure you take care of your body and mind, but be just as concerned with your essence, your soul.

71 Take (Safe) Risks

College is a time to step out, take chances, and find your true personal, academic, and professional interests. It's a time of experimentation, reflection, and affirmation.

When we hear about risk taking, it is usually associated with what are clearly negative actions. Risky behavior is often translated as experimenting with illicit drugs, driving under the influence, or having unprotected sexual relations. Those behaviors are not risky—they are downright stupid and dangerous.

Taking risks means moving out of your comfort zone. It means stretching your range of friendships, expanding your intellectual horizons, and exploring the world of opportunities that lie before you.

If you've felt terribly constrained at home and in high school, don't go to college and break out of your shell by going crazy the first week or semester. Be smart, and take your time and err on the safe side of risk taking. And if you feel the need to rebel against your parents or other authorities in your life, don't harm yourself in the process. Be smart and do better than them. Set an example by how you choose to live your life as an adult.

Did you grow up listening to a particular type of music? Rock? Rap? Country? Classical? College is a time to borrow a friend's music, go to the opera, or go to a club that plays music you've never really allowed yourself to be open to.

Do you like Italian or Mexican food? In college, try some salmon, tofu, hummus, or tea. Taste some new varieties of ice cream. Go to an Indian restaurant. Try a new salad dressing or a different kind of mustard on your hot dog.

You've spent the last four years managing the complex cliques and social arrangements of high school in order to fit in. Now relax, forget all that stuff, and be yourself. Make some new friends. Hang out with people whom it wasn't cool to be friends with in high school but who could very likely turn out to be your best friends.

Wear clothes that you like, not that your friends all wear or your parents liked. Try something bright, or a different color, or a new style. Buy a new hat or scarf.

The same is true about your academic interests. Don't just get busy filling requirements—take some courses you like. Did you always want to know more about paintings in the art museum? Study art history. Have you wanted to feel like you can understand the business section of the newspaper? Take an economics course. Was your favorite school assignment that of collecting different kinds of leaves in second grade? Then take a biology class or environmental studies or geology—all of those fields might bring you back to an original intellectual passion.

Every day on television we are faced with innumerable choices about which toothpaste or laundry detergent to use, yet when it comes to professional careers, many college students think their options are limited to business, law, engineering, and medicine. What a shame!

You get to decide what makes you happy, what gives you meaning in life, what you want to spend forty and usually many more hours of every week of the next fifty years doing. Don't let other people—be it well-meaning parents, teachers, friends, or some imaginary voices in your consciousness—tell you what to do with your life and your time. By all means, listen to these people, because they do mean well and do have your best interests at heart. But college is the time to explore a life of opportunities in any number of professions that are open to someone as bright and as interesting as you!

REBECCA FRANKEL—*"No, Thanks. I'll Pass on That."*

It was her first week of college—actually the week prior to the start of classes—and Rebecca Frankel was standing in a frat house with a drink in her hand at about two in the morning. Rebecca had come to college eager to jump into everything. She was looking forward to meeting her roommates, ready to get involved in campus activities, and excited about starting her courses.

She moved into her residence hall about ten days prior to the start of class for a busy week of activities. Rebecca went to all the events of the week, including retreats, advising workshops, book discussions with faculty, the Hillel ice cream social, and loads of late-night parties with lots and lots of alcohol. Her college offered nonalcoholic alternative activities each night, which were fun and well organized, but they weren't truly an alternative because they all ended just around the time the student drinking parties began.

Rebecca loved these activities except for the fact that she hadn't really wanted to go to the late-night parties. Rebecca had grown up learning to have fun and being involved without drinking as part of the fun. Her parents were strict about this, and she agreed with them, so in high school she had just decided not to hang out with those students who chose to drink.

She thought college would be different. Rebecca hadn't expected the social scene to include so much drinking. However, her new friends in the residence hall didn't seem to have any problem with all the drinking, and they tried to convince her to come along. Since Rebecca hadn't made friends yet, she didn't want to be left out, and so one night she decided to go out with the students from her floor.

When she arrived at the party, Rebecca was overwhelmed with the number of people there. It was a body pack. Everyone had a drink in their hands, and the guys seemed to be hitting on all the first-year women. There were kegs and punch bowls everywhere. The music was blaring, and people seemed to be having a good time.

Rebecca and the women from her floor wandered through the crowd to check out the scene. A few of the women immediately got cups of beer and began to get into the mood of the party. They invited Rebecca to join them, but she declined. Some guys came over, introduced themselves, and started talking and laughing with Rebecca's group.

This wasn't Rebecca's type of party, but she had come along and she wanted to fit in and give it a chance. She decided to take a drink after all so at least she looked like part of the party. She acted sociable, met some new guys, and introduced herself to some new women. Like most of her interactions during the week, Rebecca liked some of the people she met but did not like others so much, especially the one guy who kept trying to kiss her.

Despite giving it a try, Rebecca was very uncomfortable. She didn't object to other people drinking, but she did object to herself drinking. The whole scene just wasn't for her. This wasn't how she liked to meet and get to know people. Instead of feeling fun and relaxed at the party, she felt tense and awkward.

Rebecca was very upset but mostly with herself. She had always prided herself on being a strong and independent person, and she felt that she hadn't been that person tonight. Here she was at this party, which wasn't her kind of party, acting in a way that wasn't true to herself. "Okay," she thought, "maybe I'm being too tough on myself. It's good that I gave this a try and took a chance to see if I would like this kind of college party. But, why am I still here? And why am I holding a cup of beer when I don't like beer?"

Rebecca decided to leave the party. A couple of the women from the floor saw her getting ready to leave and joined her right away. The others stayed. On the way home, they realized that they had all felt uncomfortable at the party. As they began to relax, they started talking and sharing with each other about who they really were and what they really liked. They decided to stop for pizza on the way home and made it back to the residence hall by four in the morning.

All in all, Rebecca felt pretty good about the night. She had made some good friends and learned about campus life. Mostly, she had learned a lot about herself. She had made some mistakes, but she had also reaffirmed what she believed in and what kind of person she wanted to be. Classes hadn't even started, but she had already begun her college education.

"Don't get mono." That straightforward piece of advice comes directly from one of my favorite students. Mononucleosis should be avoided, of course. But many students get so busy with their lives that they push and push their bodies to their limit and beyond. Then, when they get mono, they are surprised that they had forgotten the straightforward advice of my wise student.

My student's advice speaks about much more than mono, however. It's all about looking after the health of your body. Feed it and sleep it and it will be there for you to fully enjoy all those wonderful, electrifying moments of college life. It will sustain you through some of the more difficult and stressful times as well. Ignore your body, and even though you probably won't get mono, you'll still have colds, be sluggish, and won't be able to participate at 100+% to do everything you want at college. Don't forget to wash your hands frequently.

Don't forget to sleep. Pretty simple advice, right? The truth is that too many students get very little sleep on a regular basis and more than a few skip sleeping entirely, more than anyone would like to think.

It's a myth that students don't go to bed in college before two in the morning or that no one starts studying till after eleven at night. Some few students do study well after things quiet down in the wee hours of the night, but most students' academic productivity and retention decreases dramatically once they get tired. This is not rocket science.

Though eating and sleeping are things you've done your entire life, in a funny way, they are new experiences at college. Cafeteria food presents great opportunities, such as plentiful food and no need for cooking and washing dishes. It also presents new challenges that may lead you to eat more than you ever wanted or less than you really need.

You may have heard about the "freshman fifteen." I think you should just follow the sound dietary advice given to everyone, either in or out of college, that you should do your best to eat healthy foods and exercise regularly. Yes, you may gain a few pounds or lose a few pounds due to all the changes when you first start college, but if you're exercising and generally making healthy choices from the array of foods in the cafeteria, you'll do just fine.

What you should concern yourself with is keeping a positive attitude and a good sense of self-esteem. It's much easier to do so when your body is getting nourished.

Don't forget to eat. Some students get so involved at exam time or during their involvement in some major campus activity that they skip meals, thinking they can get by till the next mealtime comes along. If you miss meals, you'll feel weaker, be more stressed, have less internal stamina to constructively manage all the activities in your life, and be more vulnerable to getting sick.

Don't forget to dress appropriately for the weather. If it's raining, don't worry first about fashion. Bring an umbrella or wear a raincoat. You don't want to be walking around campus soaked all day. If it's cold and snowing, don't go out in a t-shirt and shorts. Wear heavy socks, a sweater, gloves, scarf, heavy coat, hat, and some good boots. Think about thermal underwear. It's more fashionable to be healthy and participating in everything than lying in bed with a fever.

And what about when you're starting to feel a little under the weather? Again, listen to your body. If your throat is sore, drink some hot tea or orange juice and eat a bowl of chicken soup. If you're cold and it's snowing outside, dress warmly. If you're more tired than usual, get extra sleep.

You're in college—you're smart and you know all this advice. Practice it in college, and your body will thank you by working at full efficiency.

Regular exercise is good for your physical and mental health. Moving to college from high school will require you to adapt new routines and find new means to get your body moving, but be sure to keep active.

Most campuses have state-of-the-art recreational facilities, including all manner of strength and exercise machines, tracks, swimming pools, and courts for basketball, handball, and racquetball. They offer exercise classes from traditional stretching to the latest training regimens.

Many students enjoy running with friends on trails throughout the campus and on the city streets. It's a great way to be with people, get to know your way around town, stay in shape, and feel good about yourself. There are always fun and competitive races, some for pleasure and some to raise funds for good causes.

Sports and college go hand in hand. It can be great fun watching big-time intercollegiate competitions, but there are opportunities to play on competitive intramural sports teams in almost any sport imaginable. Football, basketball, volleyball, field hockey, soccer, ultimate Frisbee, golf, and skiing are just a few of the sports in which students participate. On most campuses you can choose teams that are coed, all-male, or all-female, and you can also choose to be in leagues that are more or less competitive.

Team sports are a good way to meet people, build your skills, have fun, and learn to work collaboratively with others. They are a good break from your academic focus and can give you a regular activity to look forward to and provide structure to your free time. Make sure you pick a team that you like and a sport that you enjoy. Your team sport should be fun for you, not an additional stress in your life.

By exercising your body, you will feel renewed, and you will find that your mind is refreshed as well. You will come back from exercise with some new and probably more constructive insights about conflicts you are facing, problems you need to solve, studying you need to do, and tasks you need to accomplish. It will help to reduce the clutter in your mind and allow you to move more happily and productively through your day.

74 Limit Your All-Nighters

It's not true that you must pull all-nighters to consider yourself an authentic college student.

All-nighters are not a good idea generally and certainly not a good habit to get into. Most students' attention spans and ability to focus decrease rapidly as they get tired. You are fooling yourself if you think your ability to study and retain knowledge will be effective after you become tired.

This is college, after all, and the work is difficult, complex, and challenging—even when you're at your most alert. Unfortunately, *alert* would not be the word to describe most students at four in the morning.

Rather than studying ahead of time, some students resort to drinking cup after cup of coffee to keep themselves alert and awake throughout the night. The results can be pretty ugly the day after. When you're actually taking the history exam or giving your Spanish speech at eleven, your coffee withdrawal will hit you hard, complete exhaustion will take over your body, and your mind will go limp. It's just not a winning strategy.

Worse than coffee is that some students resort to taking speed or over-the-counter medications to keep them alert through the night. This is truly a disaster in the making. The fact that you are resorting to drug stimulants for the sake of writing a paper or studying for an exam should serve as a wake-up call to you. At a minimum it's a sign that your perspective on things has become badly distorted.

If you find that you are pulling more than one all-nighter per month, you should consider going to your academic counselor to find help with study and time management skills. If you're using any controlled substances, go to health services and your counseling office immediately for confidential advice, medical attention, and support.

Remember, you're in college because you're smart, motivated, and a good student. In high school you probably complained that school should start later because you needed more hours of sleep. In college you still need your sleep. You need to sleep to remain alert and up to the challenges of college. Be smart about your study skills, time management, and physical and mental health.

75 Be Safe in Sex

Whether you're a man or a woman, straight or gay, you need to become educated about safe sex. If you don't know how to protect yourself and your prospective partner before you come to college, take the first days of college to get a crash course on the subject. You and your prospective partner's health and life depend on it.

As an adult, you will make your own decisions about whether or not to have sexual relations during your college years. The fact is, however, that large numbers of Jewish college students are sexually active and do engage in intercourse, and those who do, as well as their friends, need to know what to do to avoid unwanted pregnancy and sexually transmitted diseases.

Sexual choices are serious ones, with personal, emotional, social, and religious ramifications. Too many students are too skittish to talk about sexual relations and sex education, even though they've been exposed to TV shows, Internet videos, talk shows, and movies that seem totally consumed with sex. The consequences of unprotected sex can leave you with enduring and dangerous illnesses such as HIV/AIDS, unwanted pregnancies, and difficult personal choices about abortion or raising a child.

One of the best ways that sexually active people can avoid having unsafe sex is to remain sober. All kinds of bad judgments and ill-considered actions take place under the influence of alcohol. The likelihood of having unwanted and unprotected sex rises exponentially if you are under the influence of alcohol or other drugs.

What are some places and times that are particularly risky for the mix of alcohol and (unprotected) sex? The first days of college, before classes start, are notorious for parties with heavy drinking and upper-classmen taking advantage of first-year female students. Pregame and postgame football parties are another time to stay sober if you don't want to get into sexual trouble. Finally, students continue to tell me that some fraternities, despite annual pledges of restraint in alcohol use, remain bastions of out-of-control drinking and unwanted and unprotected sex. Beware!

Another way that sexually active people can avoid unprotected sex is to talk with their steady partners about safe sex. Be sure that both of you are committed to using protection and being safe every time you engage in sexual activity.

Go to health services and talk to a doctor, nurse, or peer health educator to learn what to do to protect yourself. Create an informal support network of friends, female and male alike, to make sure everyone in your group is well educated and has all the protective devices available.

One of my students was a varsity college football player who one year was doing community service with an organization responsible for educational outreach about HIV/AIDS. During the course of his training and subsequent educational outreach work, his awareness and concern about safe sex increased dramatically. One day he came to office hours to tell me that he realized that many of his teammates were putting themselves and their partners in jeopardy because they were so poorly educated about safe sex and because so little protection was being used. He told me that he had begun distributing condoms to the football team and asking around to see if there was interest in more education.

You should follow this student's lead. Get educated. Get condoms and other protection for safe sex. Think about these issues now, well before you find yourself in a situation when it will be that much harder to start the discussion. Find friends who care enough about you and each other to support one another to always be protected and prepared. This is everyone's responsibility: yours, your partner's, and your friends—men and women alike.

76 Control Your Alcohol Use and Don't Use Drugs

You're on your own at college. With regard to alcohol and drug use, you will be able to do pretty much whatever you choose. It is, therefore, important that you give some thought to your use of alcohol and other drugs so you make the choice that is right for you.

The question of how you want to behave in college with regard to alcohol and other drugs is not one you can avoid. Alcohol and drugs will be widely available, and there will be both friendly encouragement and sometimes pressure from friends and social organizations to drink and use drugs. In the residence halls, students you know and like will be inviting you into their rooms to drink, smoke marijuana, or try other drugs. Many off-campus parties will have alcohol and marijuana available for you to use, and many will have other substances available for you to get high.

Come to college having given some thought about how you want to act. You will be able to say yes or no as often as you want. Whether you choose to drink or not will have no impact on your involvement in most college social activities. Most of your peers will be very accepting of your decision not to drink with them, but you will need to have enough self-confidence to say no when the offer presents itself. You may also decide you want to say yes to a few drinks but also later to say no before you've had too much alcohol.

One key issue to think about is why you want to drink or use drugs. If it's because you can't feel relaxed or sociable without a few drinks in you, then maybe those social feelings are something you want to work on without the crutch of a drink. If you think your life is too boring and humdrum, that you can't experience the highs of life that others seem to have without getting high on drugs, maybe you need to examine your life so that you can experience the real joys of living when you're not drinking or using drugs.

Data on binge drinking on college campuses are now collected each year with little variation in the frighteningly high rates of bingeing. Every year, news reports tell of the high numbers of college students taken to the hospital as a result of alcohol poisoning. Despite the clever and entertaining TV and print ads glamorizing alcohol use, most people know from personal experience that people who are drunk can be gross, destructive, belligerent, and even violent. And the deadly statistics of drinking and driving as well as the dangers of alcohol and drug addiction are all well known. Finally, it's important to keep in mind state laws regarding age requirements, using a fake driver's license as identification, and possessing or selling illegal substances.

Your use of alcohol and other drugs in college is just one more decision you will need to make as a young adult. It will be your decision, not your parents', your teachers', your rabbi's, or your friends'.

It's ultimately a decision about your mental, emotional, and physical health. Understanding why, whether, and how much you choose to use alcohol or drugs will help you discover more about the life you lead, about the degree of happiness and fulfillment in your life, and what changes you might want to consider making about your very essence. These are important decisions for you as you grow and learn as a bright, independent adult. Choose wisely.

77 Lock Your Door and Don't Walk Home Alone at Night

The simple suggestions to remember to lock your door and never to walk home alone after dark aren't 100% fail-safe, but they're easy, commonsense approaches to personal safety. You ignore them at your own risk.

Most colleges, even those campuses in areas with higher crime rates, have a feeling of safety. Colleges tend to be nurturing, safe environments, with teachers, counselors, peer advisors, and friends all looking out for you. You can easily get the feeling that the worst that could befall you is a bad grade on a test or a bureaucratic person in the registrar's office who won't give you what you want.

Add to that your own sense of invulnerability that is commonplace with late teens and young adults. You're Superman, Spider-Man, and Wonder Woman all wrapped up in one.

Unfortunately, the ugly, cruel realities of life are right at the doorstep of your college campus. There are crimes of opportunity, crimes of spontaneity, and crime gangs at work. Criminals know when students move into the residence halls. Criminals know that students bring computers, TVs, and cash. They also know that students will let anyone into their residence hall and that many don't lock their doors.

If you're a criminal, or even another student who wants some good "stuff," it's easy enough to dash into a student room, grab a laptop or wallet off of a desk, and then walk down the hallway looking like any other student. It could happen in the two minutes you go next door to your neighbor's room, or it could happen in the twenty minutes that you go down to the bathroom to take a shower and brush your teeth in the morning.

Some brazen thieves will even walk into your unlocked residence hall rooms late at night while you are asleep to rob you. This doesn't happen frequently, but why risk it? All you need to do is be diligent about locking your door.

The other high crime moment is on the street after dark, particularly late at night. If you're alone on the street late at night, you're asking for trouble, whether you're a man or a woman. If you're a woman, there's also the greater likelihood that you may be the victim of a sexual assault.

Colleges have programs to warn you about these dangers and what precautions to take to be safe. They will tell you to lock your doors at all times and never to walk alone at night. Many campuses have late-night shuttle buses to take you back to your residence hall or even permit you to call campus police for a ride home. There are organized "safe-walk" programs, where you can call for a person to walk you home from late-night studying or partying. Most colleges today have emergency phones throughout the campus that connect directly to the campus police and immediately notify the police of your location.

Respect yourself enough not to let yourself get into dangerous situations. Take simple steps to minimize the odds of becoming a crime victim. Enjoy the freedom of adult independence by being smart enough to use good sense about your safety.

ALEXANDRA KRAFT—*"I Need to Take a Deep Breath."*

Alexandra Kraft was Ms. Wonderful. She had great grades, was the perfectly well-mannered young woman, popular in school, good at sports, and president of her Reform Temple Jewish youth group. Her teachers loved her intensity and commitment to her academic studies. She went above and beyond. Among her friends she was the leader of the group, always thoughtful, fun, and clear-headed. She was a winner.

At home, Alexa was surrounded by a very supportive family. Her two younger siblings looked up to her and admired everything she had accomplished. Her mother, a radiologist, loved that Alexa was so interested in science and hoped that she would go into medicine like her. Her father, a very successful corporate attorney, made sure that Alexa had every advantage one could hope for.

Expectations were sky high for Alexa and for most of her life she had flourished under the pressure of others' expectations. Now, coming to college, Alexa for the first time began to think about what she wanted for herself, both professionally and personally and what she wanted out of life materially and spiritually/Jewishly. Friends and family, all well-intentioned of course, constantly asked her about her major and her career plans. Alexa was pleased with their interest, but it also added a heavy measure of stress to her already stressed-out life.

At times it seemed like an epidemic was taking place in high school, and mostly among the girls. Although not everyone spoke openly about it, it was a fact that a great many of her friends were facing anxiety issues, depression, eating disorders, or unhealthy levels of stress. Now, approaching the first weeks of college, an exasperated Alexa, who had previously escaped the anxiety and depression that her friends had experienced, wondered if she didn't somehow deserve a break from the pressure.

"Can't I just have a moment to enjoy my accomplishments and go to class without having to worry about my next major achievement? Don't I ever get a day to live in the present and enjoy the 'here and now' without having to plan my major, my career, my family, my entire future? I need some time to relax and to take a deep breath."

During these first weeks, Alexa's parents called often to see how she was doing at college. They asked about papers and grades, praised her when she got A's but grew silent whenever Alexa announced she had received a A– or B grade on an assignment. They urged her to question her professors about anything less than A because they feared such grades would hurt her chances for competitive medical, law, or business schools. They made suggestions about courses she should take that they thought would be good for her career. They encouraged her to talk to the career center about summer internships and writing a resume. And it was still September.

Alexa loved her parents no end. And they loved and adored her. But they simply didn't understand what she was going through. They worried about her stress but also wondered why she didn't seem to be thriving. They knew she didn't sound like her usual self, but they didn't appreciate the pain she was experiencing. It was hard to live your entire life being perfect.

Alexa's RA, living on her floor close by to her room, could, however, clearly sense that something was wrong. One late night as they were talking and sharing, the RA, who herself suffered from depression since her late teenage years, offered to go with Alexa to the campus counseling center.

Alexa didn't hit it off great with the counselor, but their conversation helped her recognize that this was something she needed to address. Alexa eventually made her way to an off-campus therapist and in time talked with her parents about her seeking counseling. It took some time, but Alexa began to manage her anxiety more successfully, and found that she was better able to face the pressures of college. Alexa also began to think more deeply about the quality of her life, her values, and her ambitions for the present and the future. Her eventual openness with her parents, in a good way, also helped them feel comfortable sharing with Alexa some of their adult concerns and questions about their own lifestyle and quality of life.

This had been a very trying period for Ms. Wonderful. But Alexa felt like she had grown so much and also learned so much about herself and about life. It wasn't what she had expected from her first year of college, but she felt better prepared for the rest of her life than she had in a very long time.

78 Know How to Get Out of Dangerous Situations

The first rule of safety is that you should not put yourself in a situation that has a high potential to endanger you and others. If you don't do drugs, don't hang out with drug users or dealers. If you want to get home safely late at night, don't walk alone and don't go down dark streets. If you are sexually active but don't want to get sexually transmitted diseases, carefully protect yourself and have safe sex. If you don't want your room to be robbed, lock your door. If you don't want to cause a disastrous car accident, don't drink and drive.

The second rule of safety is to have an exit strategy if you should find yourself in a difficult or dangerous situation. Why do you need this second rule if you follow the first rule? The reason is that you can't always fully control your circumstances, try as you might. Sometimes, through no fault of your own, you will find yourself in a potentially dangerous situation.

Picture yourself going to the library one night to study for an important exam. While you don't plan to stay there very long, you find you are doing good, focused work, and before you know it, it's two in the morning and the library is closing. You quickly gather your belongings and start heading back to your residence hall. Although you've used the campus safe-walk program in the past, this time you're tired and still thinking about the exam questions, and you just start walking across campus. As you walk along, you hear some people shouting things at you. You look back and see a couple of guys you don't recognize and who don't seem friendly. You look around some more and notice that you are the only student walking along this path. Fortunately, you have your cell phone with you and have made a point of knowing where campus emergency phones are located. You know there are several phones on this path, so you hurry to the next one, stop at the phone, and make a quick 911 call. The campus police arrive in less than a minute.

You go to an off-campus party with a friend. You hear that there will be great music and dancing, and your friend encourages you to come along. He has a car, so you ride with him to see his old high school buddies. At first the party is great fun. Before too long, however, everyone starts getting high. You're not particularly comfortable with everyone using drugs, but you try to enjoy the music. As it gets later, you realize that your friend is in no condition to drive safely back to campus. You offer to drive your friend's car, but he doesn't want to leave. Fortunately, you've planned ahead for this kind of situation. You have your cell phone with you, and you carry extra money with you in case you ever need to take a taxi home. You call a taxi, and despite some uncomfortable waiting around, the taxi finally arrives and takes you back to campus.

You've been getting closer to someone you feel very attracted to. The relationship has been great in all respects, and it has not been a sexual relationship. One night you find yourself alone with this person in your residence hall room. Things move along fast—faster than you would have anticipated. You and your friend are about to make love, but you both realize that you don't have any protection. Fortunately, you've talked with friends about what you would do in this situation, so you know how you must act. Despite your desires and despite your concern that this might harm this new relationship, you firmly tell your friend that you won't have sex without protection. Your friend, to your delight, not only agrees with you but expresses relief that you stopped things before you engaged in unprotected sexual intercourse.

These kinds of scenarios or others like them do not happen frequently on campus, but they will happen. You'll be wise to recall situations you've been in where you could have used a good exit strategy and also to imagine possible scenarios in which you'll need a quick response to protect yourself. Be smart, not passive or frightened. It's just one more way to stay safe and healthy in college.

79 Get Help in Case of Emergencies

Despite all your precautions, it is possible that an emergency situation may occur during the several years that you're in college. When you lived at home, you might have depended on your parent(s) to respond in the event of emergencies. Now you should be prepared to do so, and by all means you should take action if emergencies arise.

Since it is much more likely that you will be part of an emergency involving people living around you than yourself, let's assume that the emergency you have to deal with concerns a friend of yours, not you.

One emergency situation that occurs on college campuses with some frequency is alcohol poisoning. Someone goes to a party, drinks far more than he or she can handle, and collapses. It is essential that you call 911 immediately. I have heard of students hesitating to call 911 because they feared that the police would ticket them or their friend for being a minor in possession of alcohol. In the meantime, the friend lost precious minutes of urgently needed medical attention. If you find yourself in this situation, call 911 and get help immediately!

Another type of emergency situation involves a sexual assault. Your friend will need to get help if he or she has been sexually assaulted. Medical, counseling, and criminal issues may be involved that need to be addressed. Most campuses have phone hotlines and special personnel with expertise in counseling victims of sexual assaults. In addition, most campus and city police today have officers who are specially trained to respond sensitively and thoroughly with individuals who are victims of sexual assault. The same is true at most hospital emergency rooms.

You may find yourself faced with a student you know who has a medical or psychiatric emergency. If you come upon a student who has collapsed, is having difficulty breathing, or is wounded and bleeding, immediately call 911 for emergency medical attention.

These kinds of emergency situations can often have some impact on a student's academic progress, even if it is short term. Encourage the student to contact his or her academic advisor or dean, or do so yourself. These administrators will alert the faculty that there is a legitimate reason why this student is not in class or will be turning in exams or assignments late. When the immediate emergency has passed, the student can then follow up with each individual faculty member to make whatever additional arrangements might be necessary.

For you, dealing with an emergency may be frightening, especially if it's the first time you've had to do so. You should feel confident, however, that college officials, medical and counseling staffs, and police officers are all well prepared for such situations and are there to help you out. They have considerable experience with these situations and will guide you and your friend on how to deal with the immediate emergency and any necessary follow-up.

80 Visit the Counseling and Health Centers

Your college has invaluable resources available to you to support your well-being so that you can focus on your academic studies. You should take full advantage of these resources and services because they will serve you well. Since your tuition and fees pay for these services, you shouldn't hesitate for even a second.

There are many reasons for visiting the counseling or health centers. The most obvious reason would be if you're ill or injured—if you have a fever, a sore throat, a broken arm, or a stomach flu. Go to the health center to see a doctor or nurse. They'll check your vital signs, examine you, and prescribe medications if needed.

You might also want to visit the health center if you need birth control devices, think you might be pregnant, or want to be tested for sexually transmitted diseases. You may come to college with previously diagnosed problems and need continuing treatment of headaches, eating disorders, vision problems, or depression.

Some colleges have a counseling center that is separate from the health center, but they are often closely integrated. Counseling centers schedule regular appointments but also almost always have walk-in hours when you can just drop in without an appointment and someone will be available to see you. Just like the health center, there is usually no cost or just a minimal payment to see a counselor. Several decades ago there was a stigma attached to seeing a counselor or therapist, but today quite the opposite is true.

Students go to the counseling center for a variety of reasons. You might be very homesick or might have a close relative at home who is not well and want to talk to someone about the situation. In the first weeks you might find that you are having trouble adjusting to being on your own and going to college, or your parents might call to tell you that they are filing for a divorce or that there are financial difficulties because one parent has been laid off from work. You might find yourself in a relationship for the first time and need someone to talk to about it, you might be in a relationship that is breaking up badly, or you might be in a relationship with a person who is manipulative and abusive.

Other students go to counseling or the health center to get help with eating disorders. If a student is sexually assaulted while on campus, the counseling center and health center are there to help. Some students are abusing drugs or are alcoholic, and when they are ready to seek help they may get coordinated support from both the counseling center and health center. Still other students are suicidal, and the counseling center can help them address those issues.

Sometimes, when students have academic problems, the cause may lie with issues that are not related to the classroom but need to be addressed in the counseling center. Some students have problems managing their money for the first time, and they need to talk with someone about how to get those issues, like credit card abuse, under better control.

These services are part of your college's resources. They are for you, not just for others. You pay for them, and you should take full advantage of them. If you're in doubt about whether your problem is serious enough to go to the health or counseling center, by all means err on the side of going for help. Getting routine help and support for your physical and emotional/mental health is part of growing up and becoming an adult. You're smart—use these services!

8

Mishpacha (Family), Finances, and the Details of Daily Life

81 Call Home: Ask for Care Packages, and Don't Forget Your Bubbe and Zayde

You're enjoying your independence. You may miss home, but you want to show that you can be on your own. What are the rules about calling your parent(s)? Are you supposed to? Do you have to? If you do call, how often?

Meanwhile, you're busy. You've got a million things to do. You're excited about the first days and weeks of college. There's so much going on that you don't want to miss anything. Where do the parent(s) fit in all of this?

If you are living on campus, you should make a point of staying there, especially in the first weeks of college. Some students who live relatively close to campus travel home every weekend. That choice will rob you of the opportunity to fully invest emotionally in campus life, activities, and new friends. If you are at home most weekends, then college doesn't really become home; you don't achieve the valuable growth and separation from your home and high school experience.

It's important to stay in touch with your family because they love you, and they will be a part of your life forever. Your parent(s) want to hear from you. They want to know if you're eating, staying healthy, and going to class. They are thinking about you, anxious about how you're adjusting, how you're finding the demands of college, and whether you're making friends. Even if there are issues you want to actively distance yourself from and people that you choose not to be close to, it would be an extreme case to choose to have no contact at all.

You need to decide how frequent and deep your contacts are because every student will have a different kind of relationship with their parents. Students I know have many different ties with parent(s) in college. Some students call home to talk every day, even multiple times each day. Other students send emails or talk every few days or once a week. A very small number get in touch every month or every couple of months.

You have control over what you want to talk about with your family. You can ask for advice about classes, about relationships, about campus activities, about Jewish identity issues, or about finances. Or you might decide that all you want to share with your parent(s) is that you're alive and well and doing okay. That's much, much better than having no contact.

For their part, your parent(s) may have their own problems dealing with your leaving the house. It creates significant changes for them, and they will go through an adjustment period just like you. If you're the first to go to college, it signals a period of change in their lives, that their kids are growing up, as are they. If you're the sole child in the family or the last to go to college, then your parent(s) are in for an even greater adjustment, having to renew their adult lives and their married life as a twosome, if indeed they are married, or as a single individual living alone.

So, get in touch with your parent(s). Please call your grandparents, your bubbe and zayde, because they love you and miss you a lot. While you're at it, ask them to send along a little care package. It's great to receive packages at college, whether they're large or small. Tell your parent(s) and grandparents I said so. It'll give you a lift just when you need it, and it will make your parent(s) feel like they're needed and are still helping to raise you.

82 Make Your First Visit Home a Good Experience

When you go back home for the first time from college, you want it to be a good visit. Do your part to make sure it's as good as possible.

There will be a lot of excitement on everyone's part when you go home. You will be very engrossed in all the new things you are experiencing in college and will expect everyone to pay attention to you and your new life. Because there is so much new for you—whether you've been gone a week, a month, or a semester—you will want your family and friends to listen to your every word.

Yet at home, your siblings, friends, and perhaps even your parent(s) will want you to pay attention to their experiences as well. They will feel that they too have grown, changed, and developed new interests, and they will want you to be interested. However, you are likely to feel that no one has had as many new experiences or changed as much as you have. To you, things at home might look pretty much just like you left them. In many ways, you will be right, but still you will need to be ready to listen as well as share.

You should be ready for a fair amount of adjusting on your part and everyone else's. At college you are in charge of your life, and no one is ever checking on you or questioning what you are doing with your time or your personal space. At home, however, your parent(s) are the boss, or at least they think that they are. They will expect you to eat when they eat, clean up after yourself, help out around the house, and perhaps even be home at a certain hour.

You may also find that your family is ready for you to immediately settle back into familiar family patterns. That can be very comforting and reassuring, but at the same time, you may realize that you've moved beyond your old familiar patterns. Before you left home, all the advice you had received was to go out, become adult and independent, and explore the world around you at college. Why, now, when you return home, does it seem that there is so much pressure to conform to the old family ways?

The biggest jolt and most awkward moment may come when you tell your family that you have to begin making plans to return "home" by a certain day and time. While everyone, including you, may have been able to avoid facing the reality of your new life and independence, when you begin referring to your new college as "home," reality will hit.

The truth is that you don't have to choose so fast between your college home and your family home. Enjoy them both. There will certainly be some discomfort in these awkward moments, but you should take advantage of what is so special during this transition time. You still have the love of family and friends in the ways you have always enjoyed, and at the same time that love and friendship are growing and transforming from childhood/teenage relationships to adult relationships.

So, when you do go to see your parent(s), take full advantage and pleasure in what you remember most fondly. Whether it's good talks, a good bed, good friends, or good memories, enjoy them still. But be your new self, too, the person who is a bit older, wiser, and more experienced and who is learning to be independent.

If you can effectively manage the awkward moments and negotiate some minor conflicts, you can have two homes during college, one at your family's house and one at the college campus. Make both homes your favorite places to be.

83 Keep Your High School Friends but Invest in New College Friendships

High school was hopefully a wonderful experience for you, and you have some great memories from that time of your life. Now, however, it's time to move on with the rest of your life. Still, you want to be able to hold onto the good relationships you had with your closest friends and also maintain ties with other friends and acquaintances.

Your first priority must be to establish your independence and build new friendships in college. To do this and to keep good relationships with your best high school friends, it's best to room blind. Don't choose to room with someone you know from high school. It will inhibit your freedom to expand your horizons in college, and it may ruin a good friendship.

If there's just one other student or even a handful from your high school who are attending the same college as you, it's perfectly reasonable for you to want to live in the same residence hall as people you know. However, if you know ten or twenty or fifty students from your high school who are attending the same college as you, then you need to actively and intentionally stake out your independence.

I have known far too many Jewish students who relive their high school social and academic worlds in college because they never make the transition to college. They choose to live with friends from the same high school, choose classes with high school friends, and participate in social activities with the same people. All of these choices may provide you with security, but in fact you will be diminishing your chances to explore, grow, learn, and find your adult identity during your college years. While you may think that your parents have trouble letting go and treating you like an adult, one's peers often have the greatest difficulty doing so. You'll find yourself stuck in high school all over again.

It's great fun to run into high school friends at college or to meet at a party or football game. It's a wonderful reunion. The same is true when you go home for the first time in the fall, whether it's for a weekend, the Jewish holidays, your fall break, or Thanksgiving. Enjoy your friends, share with them how you've grown, and tell them about all the new people, interesting classes, and exciting experiences you've had. Those friendships will grow and strengthen as long as you have the opportunity to grow and develop in college as an independent adult.

Seize your independence from your high school friends. Don't let the opportunity to grow socially as well as intellectually pass you by.

LAUREN GOLDSTEIN—*"Turn the Page on Today's Disaster."*

For Lauren Goldstein, it was one of those days when just everything seemed to go wrong. It was the fourth week of college. Everything had been going smoothly. Classes were challenging, but Lauren was keeping up and getting As and Bs on her papers and quizzes. Lauren had met many people and had found some girls on her floor that she could see herself getting close to.

Bobby had called late the night before. They got into a fight over the phone, and Lauren knew it was the end of the relationship. Bobby was talking about wanting to meet new people. Lauren was hurt and angry, but she didn't let on. She wasn't ready to give up on her relationship with her high school steady boyfriend, even though it was such a strain to try to maintain a long-distance relationship when there was so much new in her life at college. Still, Bobby persisted in the idea until Lauren finally caved in and tearily said they should take a break from one another and try seeing others.

Lauren cried all night and didn't get to sleep till very late—so late, in fact, that she slept through her nine o'clock English composition class. She skipped breakfast and ran across campus to her ten o'clock calculus class to take her first real test of the semester. She left the class shaking because she felt she had done so poorly. Many of her classmates were complaining that the test was unfair, that there were trick questions, and that the homework problem sets hadn't prepared them for the questions asked. The professor did not seem sympathetic.

Lauren came back to the residence hall for lunch and could barely eat. Her friends tried to cheer her up. She missed her parents and wanted to talk with them about Bobby, but she also didn't want to tell them how badly she had done on her test. She was tired and hungry and hurting inside.

After lunch Lauren went to her history seminar, her favorite class. She hardly said a word, and when the professor questioned her about one of the readings, she said something off the point and rambled along until another student interrupted. She could tell—or at least she imagined it was so—that the professor gave her a disparaging look. She knew she had sounded utterly stupid!

She decided to skip her next class and go back to her room but got soaked walking across campus in the rain. It had been a long, miserable day. Time moved so slowly. The minutes crept by. Lauren wondered what she was going to do. Maybe she had made a mistake; maybe she should transfer to a school back home.

At dinner, Jacob came over and sat next to her. Lauren really liked Jacob but hadn't let herself get close to him while she was involved with Bobby. Jacob was funny and easy to be with. He didn't make any demands on Lauren and listened to her when she spoke. Sallie, who was the silliest and nicest girl she had ever met, came over to sit with Lauren and Jacob and jumped in with the craziest and funniest story Lauren had ever heard. The story made no sense at all, but the three of them couldn't help but laugh out loud all through dinner. On the way out of the cafeteria, Sallie remembered she had picked up Lauren's paper from the English class she had skipped.

Her professor wrote on the back page of her paper, "Lauren—this is the best writing you've done this term. Your story is thoughtful, analytical, and clearly written! Great Work! A."

A few hours later, Lauren was up late studying and preparing for the next day's classes. The phone rang, and it was her mom. She had already heard that Lauren and Bobby had broken up and was worried that Lauren might be taking it hard. "Oh that," Lauren said, "I was so upset at first, but I'm moving on. I think I'm ready to meet some new guys here. It is a big deal, but not that big of a deal."

Lauren hung up the phone and wondered why her mother seemed so concerned. Things were looking up at college. Sure, things wouldn't always go perfectly, but she was an adult now, and the breakup with Bobby had happened so long ago. Life was moving forward so fast and intensely at college that there was little time to be stuck. That had all happened so long ago—well, it certainly seemed longer than twenty-four hours ago!

Tonight Lauren was thinking about Jacob, Sallie, her strong writing skills, and getting ready for her next calculus exam.

84 Make Friends with Staff in the Financial Aid Office

A college education, whether it's public or private, is going to cost you and your family an enormous amount of money. For many of you, it's money you don't have. Hopefully, you've already made the correct and necessary decision that you should not forgo a college education because of the high price tag. However, to find a way to pay for college—whether through grants, loans, work-study, or a combination of all three—you will eventually end up dealing with your college financial aid office.

Welcome to the world of bureaucracy! Beginning with the infamous FAFSA form (or whatever may replace it in the future as the financial aid process is constantly changing), you will be working with layers of organizations that provide financial aid funds. Your main contact will be your financial aid office, but along the way you will learn that the U.S. government and its various agencies, banks and loan institutions, sometimes state government, and various other offices are all part of the picture.

You and/or your parent(s) will need to be very organized about financial aid. It's a bad joke, but you almost need a college or even advanced degree to fill out these forms. It certainly may feel that way when you face all those questions for the very first time. Get all your tax documents together way ahead of time and buy some file folders to keep all the records and correspondence that will take place in the years ahead.

You need to make a point of getting to know a counselor at the financial aid office. Make these people your friends, not your enemies. Their difficult task is to make sense of the myriad rules and regulations—and they change every year—and to try to assign the proper amount of aid to each applicant. They want to award you aid if you qualify. Treat them as people, not bureaucrats, and you will have much greater success and much less frustration in your efforts.

If ever there was a time and a place to ask questions, the financial aid process and office is it. When you first start working on the financial aid forms, come to the office with your questions. When you get financial aid notification letters that are at all unclear, call the office and ask them to explain—I've seen some that were written in a language that isn't taught in any English class I've ever known.

Importantly, if you disagree with the financial aid office's assessment of your earnings or if you are concerned that the award you have received isn't sufficient, call the office. You'll probably be frustrated or discouraged (especially if you're put on hold), but don't shout at them. In almost all cases, they will be happy to review your file with you and offer various alternatives for you to think about in terms of financial aid.

During the academic year or when tuition bills arrive, if the award doesn't show up or if you haven't received the amount you expected, don't panic. Just walk over to the financial aid office to look at your file. Bring all your well-organized financial aid files with you to help make your case. In the event you need an emergency loan or if you've overspent part of your budget that should have gone toward financial aid, talk with someone in this office for advice on how to proceed.

Colleges want you to have enough funds to pay tuition. Think of them as your allies in the financial aid game. Most likely you won't get as much aid as you want or need, but the financial aid counselors want to be sure you are treated as fairly as the regulations will allow. They also want you to graduate college and have a rewarding experience. This is a very important relationship for you. Make it a good one.

85 Be Careful Using Credit/Debit Cards and Balance Your Online Accounts

Credit cards are not free money. They are not birthday gifts from a bank. They represent *your* money, and every dollar *you* spend, *you* will have to repay, often with high interest.

Credit cards, when used properly, are perfectly fine and provide an excellent alternative to carrying cash or checks with you. The problem is that college students are notorious for misusing credit cards. The challenge facing you is to manage your credit carefully and not to abuse it.

First, you should ask the bank to set a low credit limit to help you from overspending. Second, you should only spend money on credit that you have set aside in your budget to spend. You never want to pay credit card interest rates. Those interest rate payments are what ruin people. You gain the advantage over the banks if you spend only an amount that you can pay off in full with every monthly bill.

If this is the first time you've had a credit card, you may be overwhelmed by the opportunity to go online or into a store, see something you want to buy, and buy it, without paying cash, just credit. That's the trap that far too many college students (and adults as well) fall into—be sure to avoid it. If you don't have the money to pay for an item in a store or online, don't buy it. The second trap is that you are likely to forget today what you purchased on your credit last week, or even yesterday, and as a result, your monthly bill will shock you out of your mind.

Bank checks and debit cards would seem to be much more simple. You have put money in the bank and opened a checking account in your own name. You write checks and use your debit card, you keep track of the checks and the debit charges you've made in your check ledger or online, and you balance your statement on a regular basis. But sometimes what seems simple in theory isn't so simple in practice.

If you don't watch your checking balance, then you're likely to spend more than you have in the bank. The bank then will not honor your checks, and they will bounce. The bank will charge you high fees for going over your limit or bouncing checks, your credit will sink, and you'll be wasting a lot of unnecessary time on money matters instead of academic and social matters. You won't be happy.

Be sensible and attentive in your use of credit/debit cards and bank checks. Use credit cards wisely, as if they were cash in your pocket, and always pay on time. Remember to record and balance your checkbook each time you write a check, use your debit card, or have an electronic withdrawal. If you even think you might have a problem paying your bills, get help immediately from parents, college counselors, your credit card company, and the bank.

Can you imagine what it would be like to have an adult relationship with your parent(s)?

Life at home had its rules and routines. You knew where you stood in family matters. You were the child to your mother and/or father, growing up and experiencing life through the developmental stages of childhood and adolescence, but they were still always the adult(s) and you were not.

Now, in college, you are fast becoming an adult, just like your mother and/or father. It is a time when you can and should refashion your relationship with your parents from that of child to adult to that of adult to adult.

Certainly you will always be the child of your parent(s), but now it is time to start making the transition from being just the child to being the adult child, the adult friend, the independent adult in relationship with your parent(s).

This is not to say that you shouldn't still look to your parents for comfort if you're having a bad day or call excitedly to tell them that your professor praised you for completing a great lab experiment or to report that you have a new boyfriend.

This good transition is not likely to happen overnight, but you should want your relationship to take some big steps forward over the course of your college education. It will happen when you shift from having your parents make decisions for you to asking them for advice so that you can make your own decisions. It will happen when you make your own decision about your major, course choices, how to study for tests, whom to date, setting a curfew, balancing your bank account, paying your taxes, cooking your own meals, and so on.

You will see the change when you come home for vacations or when you decide to spend your vacations with your friends and not your family. It will happen when you make an important and difficult decision even though it is one that your parents would not agree with.

Not only are you growing and changing in this relationship, but so, too, are your parent(s). They may have even more difficulty with this than you do. They're not used to your not living at home or to not being able to tell you what to do, or they may think of you as a child only, not as an adult child or an adult friend.

If both of you work hard at this, as you must do with all your important relationships, you and your parent(s) will realize the beauty of your new relationship, which is more mature, equal, and meaningful. Both you and your parent(s) may have to leave some familiar history and ways of relating behind you, and you may find the path to change filled with some conflicts, disagreements, and trying to hold onto the past. In the long run, though, you will happily look forward to an ever deeper and more loving relationship in the many decades that lie before you.

87 Get a Job

There are many good reasons to work during your college years. Working to earn money to pay for college is only the most obvious.

Be careful not to work more than about twenty hours a week if you are attending college full time to avoid negatively affecting your academic performance. Ten to twelve hours per week is probably a more manageable load if you can get by financially.

Work or work-study (as part of your financial aid award) in college can take many forms, and you can learn from each job you have. Work gives structure to your life, and by working in college, you become grounded in the ways of the world yet remain largely protected from society's realities.

Work gives you a regular schedule, regular responsibilities, and clear accountability in terms of being paid hourly for doing a good hour's work. It will typically put you in regular contact with people outside your age group, which is a healthy contrast to the traditional college environment, where most of your time is spent with people who are of a very narrow age bracket.

Work also gives you a chance to be in contact with people from different social and economic backgrounds. If you work on the facilities or dining hall staff, you'll be with people who come from a range of economic backgrounds, some like your own and others from higher or lower economic classes. If you work in the hospital or a mall, you will also encounter professionals and clients who represent cross-sections of the population.

Working during college—at the same time that you're trying to figure out your identity issues, concentration/major, and career plans—allows you to try out different types of jobs. How does it feel to work in the service or retail sector, in the science lab, in the library, or as a teacher's assistant? What do you observe when you work in a doctor's clinic in a hospital, a law firm, a nonprofit organization, or for a professor doing research? These experiences will give you constructive insight, sometimes affirming and other times challenging your professional goals.

If you do not need to work for tuition, you may want to be slightly more selective about your hours and the kind of work you do. You may choose to wait to work till summer vacation or until your second year of college. You might decide to pursue an interesting internship for which you will be paid little or even nothing for your work. The luxury of not having to work doesn't mean that you should miss out on the opportunity to do so.

That's right. Think of work during college as an opportunity, not as a burden. You will learn a great deal from the experience if you take the time to reflect on it in light of your classes and personal development and values. It will prepare you for future positions and will look very good on your resume. Approach work positively. Not only will you learn and grow, but you will also be earning money to pay for college costs and, in some cases, for a little spending money.

88 Pick Up after Yourself: Do Your Own Laundry

When you move into your room in the residence hall and throw some socks on the floor, guess what? They will not move until you pick them up. When you've gone through all your shirts and underwear and your laundry bag is full, it will be up to you to find a washing machine to clean them. Want to wear an ironed blouse? Then you'll be the one ironing.

Have you ever wondered how your family's house stayed clean, how your clothes got washed and ironed before they reappeared in your closet, or how your floor got vacuumed? Hopefully, you know the answer because you were taking responsibility for cleaning up after yourself at home. If that's not the case, though, you're in for a big shock.

Learning to clean up after yourself is a valuable lesson to pick up in college if you haven't already had to learn it at home. Even if you can afford to pay a vendor to do your laundry and ironing in college, you should resist the temptation. If you live close enough to home to take your laundry home to your mother or father, don't do it except in an emergency. These are good life lessons: it is important to know how to take care of your basic needs.

Now that you are not living in your family's home, you are the king or queen of your room, and you make the rules. If you don't clean up, only you have to live with the consequences; if you wear dirty or smelly clothes, you'll be the one smelling the roses.

Of course, you may find there's more than a little peer pressure to stay on the clean and neat side of things. Your roommates, for instance, may have very different standards than you. They may strongly object to your clothes being strewn across the floor or hanging over the couch and desk chairs. Don't be surprised if they find it gross when you don't throw out your moldy cheese in the refrigerator or you leave your cereal bowl, silverware, and glasses in the sink unwashed. At the same time, they might also object if you're the opposite extreme and you vacuum and dust each day and complain when they don't fold their clothes neatly or make their beds.

Your personal habits quickly become everyone's business on the floors and suites of the residence hall. Your peers will know more about your personal habits than you ever wished, and they'll talk about them. Peer pressure can be far more powerful than your father or mother asking you to clean up your room.

Most important, however, is that you realize that you are responsible for taking care of yourself. As an adult, the responsibility for how you look, how your clothes appear, and how clean or dirty you keep your room is all yours. Your choices in these matters reflect on you and give people instant impressions about how you think about yourself. They will affect your relationships with roommates and friends and your own self-esteem and self-worth. It's part of becoming an adult.

DEANNA NEWMAN—*"Should I Go Home for Rosh Hashana?"*

Deanna Newman prides herself on her independence. She loves her family but was very clear that she wanted to go away to college. She wanted to experience new things, new people, new surroundings, and especially some distance from her family.

When Deanna's parents dropped her off at the residence hall at college, she kissed them good-bye and firmly told them that she would be the one to initiate phone calls and email messages. Her parents were great, but her mom had a tendency to be over-involved, and her dad had always had too many rules and instructions when she lived at home. Deanna wanted to be on her own, without her mother knowing all the details of her life and without her father telling her what classes to take and when to be at home at night.

The first few days at college, before classes began, were somewhat lonely for Deanna. Sure, everyone was very friendly and nice, and there were lots of social activities, but there was also lots of dead space when she had nothing to do. It was ironic, but Deanna kind of missed her mother's questions about whom she was hanging out with and what her plans were. But Deanna held tough and didn't call home. Instead, she acted the part of the happy, carefree college student. Deanna went to the bookstore and bought her course books, opened a new bank account, and began to find her way around campus with some of the students from her hall.

After a week at college, Deanna called home. Her parents were so excited to hear from her, and Deanna, too, was delighted to talk with them. They talked for a long time, and everything seemed great. But then her mom started to ask what seemed to Deanna like too many personal questions, and her dad started up with his list of rules. Deanna ended the conversation somewhat abruptly. She felt great about being in touch with her parents but also a little bitter that they seemed just like from before she'd left home. Deanna was changing, and she had been on her own for a full week. Weren't her parents going to change, too?

Deanna's parents were pressuring her to come home for Rosh Hashanah, and part of her really wanted to be at home for the holidays, too. It seemed like it would be so sad not to be with family, the apples and honey, and her bubbe's delicious brisket on such an important holiday. Still, Rosh Hashanah fell midweek, starting Tuesday night, and it would be so disruptive to leave school. Most of the Jewish students were staying on campus for the holidays this year because of how they fell during the week. Hillel was offering all kinds of holiday meals and services and a new friend had invited her home for the first night. Deanna decided to stick it out. She got a chance to meet some other Jewish students whom it turned out she really liked.

The first weeks of college went reasonably well, but Deanna missed home a lot. She was surprised that she would miss her parents. She called home every week, and her conversations with her parents were both comforting and annoying. Deanna's parents told her they were really trying to respect her independence, but they certainly missed her and found it difficult not to talk more often.

Deanna was torn—on the one hand she missed her parents enormously, but on the other hand, she had promised herself that it was best to be independent.

Deanna's next-door neighbor in the dorm took the exact opposite approach. Jennifer flew home for Rosh Hashanah and seemed to travel home every few weeks. She had no problem with her mother calling the Housing office to take care of her roommate conflicts and the dorm food, and rumor was that her father had even called one of her professors to complain about a midterm grade. Just the thought of her parents calling one of her professors simply horrified Deanna, and she wondered if maybe there was some middle ground that she should explore.

She decided on a compromise. There really was no reason that she couldn't talk to her parents more than once a week. "Maybe I'm being too rigid," she thought to herself. "Why can't I call home when I feel like I want to talk with them?" So Deanna decided to wait till Thanksgiving to go home to see her parents but called home and texted whenever she felt like it. Her parents, after a time, also got permission to call and email when they needed or wanted to, and everyone began to adjust their relationships so that they were more adult and reflected a transition from their parent-teenager home of the past few years.

Even though it hadn't been the easiest first months at college, Deanna was very pleased with herself. She was learning to live independently, including taking responsibility for both the good and bad that went along with that. Deanna was growing up, becoming independent, and she was really excited to be at college.

89 Show Up to Class

Yes, it's important to go to class in college. In fact, you should plan to attend every scheduled class session. It is your choice to attend college, and it is the opportunity of a lifetime. You should take advantage of every chance you have to learn.

As a person who is attending college, you obviously were a good student in high school and rarely missed classes. However, if you did purposefully miss class in high school, besides legitimate reasons like sickness or holidays, you probably felt that skipping class was a sign of rebellion or independence. School was a requirement; it was something you had to attend because someone else wanted you to, so by not going to class you were harming someone else, not yourself.

You need to think about college quite differently. To be worthwhile, college has to be *your* choice. If you don't want to be in college, then by all means save yourself and your parent(s) a lot of money and time and take a leave of absence. However, as long as you are in college, you should remember that each course you take holds immense possibilities, and you should want to be there for each session.

Most of my students do attend class every session. But I have had some students tell me that they will have to miss class because they have to rush their sorority, or they are in the midst of organizing a campus event, or are having difficulty waking up in time for a ten o'clock class. These students are attempting to be polite and respectful by telling me about their absences in advance. However, I am always struck by these excuses because it tells me that these students have badly misplaced their priorities for college.

Rushing a sorority may be important to you, but as a priority it should come after your academic work. It's very important to be involved in extracurricular activities, but you have to keep in mind which college activities are central and which are *extra*. Staying up late at night is a college rite of passage for many, but it's no substitute for being able to get up in the morning to go to class. You can't learn from class if you don't attend because you've overslept.

Embrace the opportunity you have to attend college. Be sure to take advantage of every opportunity available to you. But keep your eye on the academic prize, even while you get involved in the whole of the college learning experience. The first step is to attend classes.

90 Enjoy Your Personal Technology and Social Networks Responsibly

By the time you go from start to finish reading this one tip, the best advice on which computer, which cell phone, and which other high tech equipment to buy or use will have likely changed three times. It will also change multiple times during your college years.

That's the good news—that you are living in a time of enormous technological changes that we all hope will be used to further knowledge and advance the quality of life for everyone. What this means for you is that you must be technologically savvy and feel right at home with your laptop, phone applications, music, video, etc. Technology is re-shaping our intellectual worlds, our social networks, and our global community, and you are right in the middle of this revolution.

While college campuses do have public workstations and most space is wireless, if at all possible financially you should bring your own laptop and think of the public sites as complementary to the capabilities of your computer and other personal technology.

Talk with the advising office and orientation staff to learn if they have any specific recommendations for technology purchases. Check to see if your university offers any bargains on purchases of computers, clickers, and other technology devices, as well as repair services.

You will quickly discover that, at least in some areas, you are as current on technology developments as many of the faculty and staff on campus. And, if you are not, you should get up to speed immediately. If you haven't had the same access to technology for educational and networking purposes as your peers, then ask lots of questions, experiment, and hang out with your new friends so you become familiar. Most colleges offer tech help from staff at the library, public work stations, and even in the residence hall. Ask away.

Of course, you must be open to learning the newest innovative trends in technology for learning, studying, networking, and research. But you should also be open to your college's particular technology systems even if they seem slow or outdated. Even if some of your faculty and administrators are using networking tools that seem passé to you, you need to be in regular contact with them so don't shut off those communication pathways just because you've moved on to the next best device and network and they're still using older technology. Use the "both/and" principle and keep in mind that communication with your faculty and administrators is essential, regardless of the means.

As for social networking, embrace it, have fun with it, use it for its potential for personal, professional, and political opportunities, but understand the possible dangers and downsides of an increasingly open, networked global society. Your high school friends, your new friends at college, even the overall campus environment may make you feel as if the world is a trusting place. And, hopefully, your world is always that way. However, the networked technological world includes lots of sinister people with nothing but evil on their minds. Whenever you are contemplating sharing personal or financial information about yourself or friends, keep in mind that those folks are lurking on the same network sites. So please, please, protect yourself, your personal information, and your privacy. Beyond these criminal figures lurking online, there are also well-meaning adults and professionals in your life whom you really don't want to let know about your every mood, intimate relationship details, or behavior that is, let's say, less than family-oriented or professional.

Finally, as technologically networked as you may be, be sure you learn how to be effective personally, educationally, and face-to-face in your communication and networks. Don't interrupt conversations to take a phone call. Don't send text messages while talking with faculty during office hours. Don't go online to social network sites during class. Be as personable, confident, and sensitive making connections and sharing when you are in the moment and in the physical space of others as you can be when you are in the virtual world.

91   Get Around Town without a Car

A significant number of students coming to college have had access to cars—either their parents' cars or their own—while in high school. Yet most colleges, except, of course, for commuter campuses, require or advise students not to bring cars to college, especially during the first year. You might be wondering how you're going to manage without one or even whether you should try to ignore your college's advice and bring one anyway.

The reason for college rules about cars is the lack of parking on college campuses. Whether your college is an urban campus or is in a small town or rural area, parking is at a premium. One of the most common themes across college campuses is the universal complaining—not only by students but even more so by faculty and staff—about the high cost and limited availability of parking spaces. Everyone's unhappy.

The best way to get your mind around the no-car problem is to think of this as a liberating and green opportunity rather than as a burden or punishment. If you're attending an urban college, then hopefully your city has a great public transportation system.

Many other campuses are relatively self-contained or are located in small towns or cities. Restaurants, shopping, movies, concerts, and so forth are all within walking distance of your residence hall room. You will love the freedom of walking or bicycling to where you need to go. It's good exercise, invigorating, energizing, healthy, and much more social than riding alone in your car.

There are times, however, when you will really need or want a car to get off campus. What will you do in these situations?

Fortunately, there are some relatively easy answers to these problems in most cases. Some more isolated campuses provide shuttle buses for students to go to places of high demand, such as a mall or a metro stop. At peak travel and vacation times, most campuses have private or public transportation available for students to get to the airport or train station. Almost all campuses that are not near public transit provide students with van or car transportation to community service-learning locations.

Finally, even when your campus lacks a first-rate metro system, most towns have limited bus and taxi service. Learn to use the local bus system. And learn to pedal—bikes are great modes of transportation—just remember to wear a helmet.

Not having a car saves a lot of money, too. You won't have to make car payments or pay for gas or insurance. It also saves the environment. All the pollutants emitted by cars are reduced by each of the thousands of students who have had to leave cars at home while they are in college. So you're not only doing yourself a financial favor, you're also helping to save the planet!

9

Mazel Tov!
Looking beyond the First Year

92 Identify Faculty Who Will Write Recommendation Letters for You

Every job, internship, and graduate school will ask you to provide references. After you're in college, it will no longer be good enough to get a letter from your favorite high school teacher, the manager of the store in your local shopping mall where you worked, your rabbi, or a friend of the family who has seen you grow up and flourish.

Faculty members (and graduate student instructors) at your college will be the most important source of recommendation letters for you during your college years and beyond. You will find that you need these letters as early as your first and second years of college. If you are looking for a summer internship, a research assistantship, acceptance to a study abroad program, or a job in the library, you will be asked to provide a letter from a faculty member on your campus.

Later, when you apply to graduate school or a professional school program, it is critical that you can turn to at least two or three faculty members who will write outstanding letters on your behalf.

Most faculty will be more than willing to write one or even multiple letters for you, but only if you have developed a relationship with them or have caught their attention through your comments in class discussion, by writing an exceptional paper, or by visiting office hours.

A small number of very special faculty, usually those who have been so impressed with you that they are willing to serve as your champions, will go out of their way and initiate calls and contacts on your behalf. They will keep you in mind when they hear of scholarship opportunities, summer internships, special study programs, and research assistantships. They will make it their business to be sure you get into the best graduate programs.

Some faculty will be willing to write letters but will not be reliable about deadlines. You need to keep tabs on whether the letters you have requested have been submitted in a timely manner. If you can't depend on a faculty member to write a letter for you on time, then you are better off finding a replacement.

When you do ask for a letter, you want to make the process as easy as possible for the faculty member. If you like this professor so much that you are asking for a reference letter, it's likely that many other students are as well, and your letter is just one of several that the professor is writing. Tell your professor what jobs, programs, or graduate schools you are applying to and give him or her a copy of your resume, a statement of purpose if available, any forms that need to be filled out (usually you will have to complete part of the forms), a short written reminder about the purpose of the letter, and the due date. If it's possible to send the letter via email or through a website, ask your professor if he or she would prefer to send a letter this way or by snail mail. If the latter, include a stamped, addressed envelope for the professor to use. Let your professor know the eventual outcome of your applications—he or she will be interested to hear.

The key to asking for reference letters is to know faculty well enough that you can approach them. Your first task in securing references as a first-year student is building your relationships with faculty. After you've done that, don't be shy about asking for letters. Faculty will be pleased and honored that you have asked and will be eager to learn that you have succeeded in your job search or pursuit of advanced graduate and professional degrees.

93 Explore Possible Majors

Sometime during the sophomore year (or sooner), most colleges will ask you to declare your major or concentration. Some students come into college very certain about what they want to study. Most, however, come to college wanting to explore a wide range of subject areas and topics and are undecided about a major.

Students who have already decided their field of study prior to coming to college may have applied and enrolled in schools such as art, engineering, or nursing. Even within those schools, however, students will need to make decisions about subfields of study during their undergraduate years.

Another group of students who often appear certain about their choice of major are those who are considered preprofessional. Students who plan to attend law school often major in political science, and those interested in a career in business often choose economics. These students limit their choice of majors as a result of the widespread myth that it's essential to have those particular majors in order to gain admission to law or business school, respectively. That is simply not the case. Choose a major in a field that you find stimulating, not one that holds little or no interest for you.

Students planning to apply to medical school are required to complete many prerequisites during their undergraduate studies. Unlike their preprofessional peers in law and business, many of these highly competitive students feel pressured to double- or triple-major in order to look good on their medical school applications, so they choose to major in a science discipline like biology as well as a discipline in the social sciences or humanities. It's not necessary for you to double-major, but at least for these more narrowly focused students, it allows them to get a broader liberal arts education.

The largest group of students arrive at college undecided about their major. For most undergraduates, I think that's the preferred approach.

College is intended to be a time of exploration. Most high school curricula provide little opportunity to even begin to imagine the vast world of ideas and fields of study. Both preprofessional and undecided students are well known for changing their minds about their major multiple times during their college careers. Don't think of that as a problem. It's a natural step in the decision-making process as you take intriguing courses in new fields and then begin to pursue those subject areas in greater depth.

As a first-year student you should attempt to take courses in a wide variety of fields, and you should take those courses whose descriptions you find most interesting—or, even better, with professors who've been recommended to you as excellent teachers. You will also feel some pressure to complete general education or distribution requirements during your first couple of years. Rather than feeling overwhelmed, you should take a strategic approach, trying to fulfill your own mission of exploring broadly while also fulfilling your college's requirements. If your college has a good general education or distribution program, this should be a very easy task, because the general education requirements will overlap to a large extent with your own choices.

In your first year of college, keep your focus on exploration and breadth. Carry the idea of choosing a major in the back of your mind, but don't stress about it. It's a long way from your first semester till the time you decide on your major. Enjoy this stage of your college education, when you have the chance to take outstanding courses in the widest variety of fields.

94 Turn the Sophomore Slump into a Great Opportunity

It happens. The sophomore slump is for real. Your first year of college is an adrenaline rush, filled with new courses, new people, new activities, and a tremendous surge of independence.

Sophomore year comes along and most students expect the rush to carry them, just like the first year. The problem is that eventually the rush dissipates, your energy dwindles, and the forward thrust of your first year of college slows down, often dramatically. It's not that anything negative takes place, just that the surge of excitement of all the newness and independence begins to wear off.

The challenge of the sophomore year is to learn from all your new experiences and to begin to take control and responsibility as an adult for your independence and your choices, academic and otherwise. The rush of the first year of college must now be transformed into intrinsic motivation and commitment about your choices as an adult. The excitement and enthusiasm that reflected your adrenaline rush must now be sustained as part of your continuing approach to academics, social experiences, and the rich and full life that lies ahead of you.

The sophomore slump does happen to many students, it's not a myth. For some it will come earlier in the year and for some later. You may feel good about everything but just more sluggish. You may still like all the courses you're taking but find it's harder to do all the reading. You may be involved in great organizations but experience less of a thrill in taking on loads of responsibility.

I don't know if you can avoid the sophomore slump altogether, but you can certainly minimize the experience. The first step is for you to acknowledge the likelihood that you will experience a slump in your second year. The second step is to plan for some new challenges and experiences for your second year and to identify those continuing practices that were most meaningful to you in your first year.

What new challenges might you take on in your sophomore year? You could sign up for a new research project or a study abroad experience. You might decide to take on a leadership role in a campus organization to further develop your skills. You could look forward to a new living situation with friends or even to expanding your current group of friends. You might look forward to taking some new courses, either because you've completed the necessary prerequisites or because you now know which are the best professors and you want to study with them. Maybe what you need to do to minimize the slump is play a sport or pick up a musical instrument or plan for a great summer internship.

All of these choices take you a step beyond your first-year experiences, presenting you with new and stimulating personal, social, and intellectual challenges. They will make the sophomore year different from the first year of college, and you will feel confident that your life as a college student and adult will be new and interesting every year. You will have taken control and responsibility for your education and life path to an extent that you couldn't have imagined just a few years ago. This is no slump; you're living a great life.

JOSEPH SCHNEIDER—*"The Jewish Insider/Outsider"*

Count him in! Joseph Schneider was an involved Jewish high schooler. He attended Hebrew School right through 12th grade, was confirmed, and won awards from his synagogue. He attended Jewish camp for several summers and loved it. He had visited Israel with his family. Being Jewish was a core component of his identity.

Joe didn't need too much encouragement from his parents to attend the first Hillel welcome event. He was excited to see who was there and was interested in getting involved. But it didn't feel exactly right to him. Or maybe it felt too right, in the sense that he wanted something new and different and this seemed too much like high school.

Joe tried services on Rosh Hashanah and Yom Kippur and even attended a Shabbat dinner. Everyone was welcoming and many of his friends were there, but Joe was searching for a new level of Jewish commitment and spirituality. Some of his friends encouraged him to try Chabad, but he felt uncomfortable about their approach to gender roles. There was another group or two on campus that seemed really well-funded, but it bothered Joe that they wouldn't be upfront about what their "agenda" was or who they represented when they said they were reaching out to all Jewish students.

Joe closely followed Israel events in the news and on campus. But he was frustrated with the constant feuding among the Jewish groups especially, and the same old arguments he would read in letters to the student newspaper by Jewish and Arab students. He could still smell the foods and hear the sounds from his trip to Israel but he was tired of the endless conflict and fighting in the Middle East and the debates at home didn't seem to go anywhere.

Joe made Friday night dinner with friends and organized his Jewish camp friends to come together for singing and memories.

He only went to services on an occasional basis, usually when he was specifically asked to read Torah or lead services, but he did take an advanced Hebrew class and was considering gaining fluency in Hebrew in addition to Spanish.

Overall, Joe had a great first year in college. He made loads of friends, Jewish and non-Jewish, and even participated in an interfaith dialogue. He got involved in community service activities and started writing for a campus literary journal. Interestingly, most of his stories had a Jewish theme to them. He did very well academically, was hired as a research assistant, and kept up with his soccer playing. He even started a student sustainability group that, for Joe, grew out of his Jewish commitments. He was happy to see that there were a large number of Jewish students involved in "green" issues who helped him build the organization.

Sometimes Joe worried about how less involved he was in the Jewish organizations on campus compared to high school and what a change it was for him. Did his lack of involvement say something about him or about the Jewish organizations? Maybe the answer was, "neither." But Joe wasn't too worried about it. With his naturally contemplative and activist ways, he felt more spiritually connected Jewishly than he had been for awhile, and he also felt as Jewishly-identified as ever.

Even though Joe felt less involved and something of an outsider to organized Jewish life on campus, it was clear to others that Joe was clearly in the mix of Jewish student leaders on campus. Because of camp and his various activities, it seemed like most Jewish students and faculty on campus knew him very well. The Hillel Director noticed Joe wasn't participating in many of the activities at Hillel and asked Joe to meet with him for coffee. Joe really appreciated the outreach and conversation because rather than try to make him feel guilty, the Hillel Director actually told him he respected the fact that Joe was finding his own pathway to a meaningful Jewish life.

Joe told him about his desire to move to a deeper spiritual level in his Jewish life, and together they brainstormed some possibilities for a study group or an alternative minyan.

Joe felt good about his Jewish place. OK, he wasn't really one of the Hillel in-crowd even though he knew all those students. And even though he wasn't really sure what his next step was, he had a great circle of Jewish friends with whom he could celebrate Shabbat, and he was pursuing intellectual and social activities on campus that were meaningful to him as a Jew. Now he could envision new possibilities for exploring a more spiritual path within Judaism.

95　Spend Your Summers Productively

In high school, summer meant time for vacation and work. Your parent(s) chose your vacation—to an amusement park, to a swimming pool, to visit relatives, to camp, or traveling cross-country. Your work was based on what was available in your hometown, perhaps selling clothes at the mall, waiting tables at the diner, being a lifeguard at a local pool, or doing office work for a family friend.

In college you will have much greater control of your summer choices, and the opportunities are plentiful. If possible, it's good to be strategic about your summers, because there are a very limited number of them during the college years.

Sometimes the best choice, if you've had a very intense academic year, is to take some time off to do nothing. Clear your head, get some sleep, rest your body and your brain. That's a reasonable plan, at least for a week or two. After that, you'll find yourself extremely bored with yourself and increasingly annoying to your family and friends.

Colleges offer all kinds of stimulating summer learning programs. There are study abroad opportunities and research assistantships with faculty on campus or abroad. Some college departments have special field classes, such as literature and creative writing programs at camp-like sites off campus or geological or oceanographic expeditions to interesting sites in the mountains or oceans.

Some students choose to stay on campus during all or part of the summer rather than return to their parents' homes. They may, of course, enroll in regular summer classes. Most students who stay on campus look for cheap housing but also want to make money to pay for summer expenses as well as for expenses during the coming year. There are jobs at local businesses but also opportunities to work on campus in research labs, in residence hall kitchens, in orientation programs, giving campus tours, in libraries, and doing groundskeeping work.

Many students return to their parents' homes during the summer. They may wish to be back at home with their families, but they also try to maximize their summer earnings by not paying for room and board. At home, they may continue to work at jobs they held during high school or to return as counselors to camps they had attended when younger. Other students, particularly in professional schools, get help finding well-paying summer work related to their engineering or business studies.

Internships in your projected professional field are another great use of your summer time. Your college may be able to help you find internships, but you should plan on doing the bulk of researching what's available and asking for and filling out applications on your own. Internships may be paid or volunteer—be sure to ask. You might work in a state or national governmental office, a nonprofit agency, a business, or an environmental organization.

It's important that you think ahead about your overall summer plans during college and plan ahead early each year to be sure you can actually find the job, internship, study abroad program, or whatever that you are seeking. It's good to take at least a short break from your studies and to get some physical distance from your college campus at some point during the summer. In addition to all the exciting summer opportunities that await you, you definitely want a chance to get refreshed and renewed before you return for the next year of academic studies.

96   Investigate Internships

One of the best opportunities you can pursue during your college years is an internship experience.

Internships provide you with invaluable work experience in a field of interest to you. They give you an insider's view of what it means to come to work every day in a professional organization and field that you may wish to pursue throughout your career. Even if you choose an internship that is not in your chosen field, it will give you firsthand insights about a field that you would otherwise know only through books, the Internet, and word of mouth.

It takes a lot of time and effort to secure a summer internship. Start early. Begin working on this early in the fall semester if you hope to have an internship the next summer. You first need to investigate what opportunities exist in fields that hold some interest for you. Then you need to learn more about what qualities are desirable in an intern. You will want to update your resume and revise it numerous times to fit the specific needs of the various internships to which you are applying. Write a letter that explains both your interest in the internship and the qualifications and skills that you will bring to the position. You will need to send out many letters and make many calls to hope to be offered even one internship opportunity, but one is all you need.

Your academic department or campus career center also will likely assist you in identifying internship programs. They may have specific internship programs in governmental offices in your state or in Washington, DC, or in industry, engineering, or nonprofit organizations. Take advantage of whatever programs or advice these offices have to offer you.

Internships may be paid, unpaid, or for college credit. Some organizations may have one paid internship position and several unpaid positions. If you need to earn money in the summer, then be sure to apply only to those that offer paid internships, and keep your options open to paying positions instead of an internship. Some government, foundation, and corporate programs pay a generous stipend for full-time summer internships at designated nonprofit service organizations, for research, or in corporate offices. A few internships will offer free or inexpensive housing for their interns, but others will require you to pay for your own housing in addition to volunteering your time. Most internships do expect you to volunteer your time in exchange for giving you the rich organizational experience you will receive.

In addition to all the education you will receive, if you do an outstanding job at your internship, your supervisor will serve as an excellent reference for you when it is time for you to go on the job market. Some interns impress their supervisors so much that they even get hired at that office when they graduate college.

Do consider spending one of your summers working in an internship. You will enjoy the overall experience and the people you work with, and you will learn invaluable lessons from both the positive and the negative aspects of the experience.

College is one of life's great experiences. However, if you can manage it, limit this great experience to four years and move on to life's next great adventures. Doing so will also save you a bundle of money.

There are certainly many good reasons to stay in college beyond four years. One reason is financial need, which can force you to postpone your education because you cannot afford to pay for college expenses. A second reason is that you are working or supporting a family and cannot afford, financially or in terms of time, to attend school full time. A third good reason is that you or family members have health problems that require you to care for yourself or others. A fourth good reason is that you change your major and require additional time to complete your degree or preprofessional requirements. A fifth good reason is that you received an inadequate education in high school and consequently spent part of your first year in college taking remedial courses, slowing down your progress toward your degree.

Some students are delayed in their progress toward their degree because their college does not offer a sufficient number of courses in required fields each semester to allow all interested students to complete their degree requirements in a timely fashion. If that's your situation, you should complain to your institutional leaders—that's not acceptable.

You should make the most of your college education in a timely fashion. There is a rhythm and a community to a four-year college education. If you stay much beyond your fourth year, you will begin to lose your sense of a scholarly community and move toward a modality of course fulfillment and completing credits. Those are the necessary instrumental mechanisms of a college degree, but alone they do not represent a vibrant intellectual community.

Some students change their majors several times or are not certain about a professional path. That's fine; it's not a problem. However, if you are in this situation, you should try to complete your degree within five years. If your fifth year of college study brings greater clarity to your direction, then taking that extra year will have been a good choice.

Sometimes you will find that the key to the puzzle of discovering a compelling direction will be found more easily outside of college. If you haven't found your way early in college or still have no direction after a fifth year of college, you should begin exploring unfinished questions outside of the college arena. You may want to take a year off to travel, work at different types of jobs, or get on-the-job training with a corporate business. Within a year or two, you should have a better idea of what field interests you and what you want to pursue as you complete your college degree.

Set four years as your goal for completion of your degree, and focus your efforts on realizing all the benefits of college within that time frame. Be attentive to course requirements and consult regularly with your academic advisor. You may have good reason to extend your education beyond four years, and you shouldn't stress about doing so, but to the extent that you have control over matters, get the most out of these four years and be done. As wonderful as everyone hopes that college will be for you, there are great things ahead of you beyond college.

98 If Necessary, Look Into Transferring to Another College

You may find that you are one of those students who wants or needs to change schools after your first or second year of college. Any number of reasons might require you to consider transferring to a different college. Examine this possibility carefully, thoughtfully, and dispassionately so that you make the best decision, and be sure to keep your options open as you begin the process of applying to other schools.

You may find that you're not happy at the college you are attending or that you're reasonably happy but not fully satisfied with your educational and social experience. In either case, you want to carefully examine the reasons why that's the case. Changing colleges is a perfectly reasonable option, but you want to be certain it's the right choice for you.

You may find that the college you are attending is not the right fit for you. You should be sure that your feeling is persistent, that your unhappiness is not a reaction to one particular incident or event, such as a bad roommate situation, a low grade on a test, a professor's critical comments in class, being rejected for a part in a play, or not getting bids to join any fraternities. These circumstances and others like them can make you feel like you're not wanted at this college. However, you want to ascertain whether they are indicative of a campus culture that is not a good fit for you overall or whether you will be able to get past these unhappy moments to enjoy all that is good about the environment.

Some students are better suited to a larger or smaller campus in contrast to their present location. Other students want a college that is more or less academically intense and challenging, is more or less traditional, or has more opportunities in the arts, music, or sports.

Another possibility is that the discomfort you feel at school has more to do with your personal development and your ambivalence about what you want from the college experience. Sometimes students who are unhappy or unfulfilled at college are at a point in their lives where they need to do more self-reflection and introspection. Their unhappiness stems less from the college they are attending than other personal or external issues in their own lives. In those cases, it's better to stay put and keep making forward progress in your education while you take time to address these other issues or just to take a year off from college till you feel you want and are ready to return.

Many other reasons also lead students to consider transferring. Changes in one's family—through death, illness, divorce, or a job loss—may require a move to a less expensive college or one closer to home. Some students may decide they wish to live closer to their parent(s) or to a partner they see as a future spouse. Some colleges may not have adequate child care or may not be hospitable to students who work all day and need to take evening courses. Other students dislike a particular college's size (too large or too small) or environment (urban or rural). Some students of color and other under-represented students find a particular campus climate inhospitable, and others dislike the lack of diversity.

Transferring to another college is a perfectly reasonable option, but don't act precipitously if you're thinking about transferring. It can be a good and necessary choice for you, but take your time to decide. You can apply to transfer to other colleges without dropping out of your current school. That will buy you time to see if the negative impressions and difficult circumstances persist throughout the school year.

Whatever college(s) you attend as you pursue your degree, you want to have a rewarding and fulfilling experience. Be sure changing colleges will help you achieve that goal.

ALLISON STRAUSS—*"What Should I Be When I Grow Up?"*

For a year now, everyone—her parents, her friends, her teachers—had been asking Allison Strauss where she intended to go to college. The attention was initially very nice, but then her neighbors, her aunt whom she hadn't talked to in three years, people in stores whom she didn't even know—everyone seemed to want to know where she was going to attend college. What a relief it was when she finally was able to answer this question!

But by the time summer rolled around, Allison started to hear a new question over and over again, and it just about freaked her out. People now wanted to know what she was going to do with her life after college! They wanted a quick answer about her career plans. "All of these questions about my career," Allison thought, "and I haven't even attended my first day of class yet!"

Allison knew what people wanted to hear. Her father was a well-known corporate attorney, a senior partner in a prestigious law firm. Everyone was hoping and even expecting, actually, that she would one day join her father's law firm.

Allison, in fact, had thought about her career during her life. At different times she had wanted to be a schoolteacher, health care worker, and tennis superstar. The problem was that she had thought about most of these career options when she was less than ten years old and, as far as tennis was concerned, it was clear she'd be spending more time in front of her TV watching the sport and eating snacks than receiving a paycheck for playing.

Oh, yes, she also had law in the back of her mind, too.

However, the last couple of years Allison had been focused on friends and college. She'd worried about taking the right courses, studying, getting good grades, enduring standardized tests, and, most recently, filling out college applications. Now that she had chosen a college, she had thought she would have a chance to rest, relax, and not think about any big questions. So the questions about a career came as one big, unexpected, and unwelcome surprise.

When Allison arrived at college, she found a mixed bag of ideas about careers. A good number of students could name their intended career areas—business, law, health care, engineering. Those were some of the big ones. A few even reported that they had known what careers they wanted since elementary school and, remarkably, still wanted to pursue that goal. But Allison soon learned that most students changed their minds quickly and frequently, even during the first semester of college.

Most of Allison's academic advisors and professors counseled against making a career choice too quickly. They pointed out that college is a time to take time, to think through one's professional and career goals as an adult, and to explore broadly one's likes and dislikes. They spoke of finding out about one's self, identity, skills, and interests—particularly those that could be sustained over time. This was comforting.

However, some preprofessional academic programs required students to get on track early in college. Some students were busy taking their premed, engineering, or prebusiness courses right away, in their first semester of college. But Allison understood that many other students who were interested in business, law, education, and so on planned to take a liberal arts curriculum and pursue those more focused career pursuits later on, as juniors and seniors; through their majors; via internships; or in graduate school. The premed and engineering students, she learned, had less flexibility than others, but they also had a lot more opportunity to take a range of courses than they had believed when they first started college.

Allison took a deep breath. She knew she was a responsible person. She knew, too, that even though law was definitely an option and a great opportunity, she really didn't know what she wanted to do for her professional career. She decided to take her time to adjust to college and do well in her studies. There was so much exciting about college that she didn't want to miss. Great courses and faculty, midnight conversations, concerts, parties, new relationships, extracurriculars, study abroad, internships—she was looking forward to all of this.

Along the way, Allison was certain she would begin to find her direction, her goals, her passions, and her career. Allison knew where the career center was located and would find her way there when she was ready. She also knew where her father's law firm was located if she wanted to talk with anyone there. For now, she was going to think about her first semester of college and leave the rest of her life for a little later down the road.

99 Take a Summer Vacation

It's important that you take vacations, enjoy them, and put your academic work behind you for the time that you have off.

The culture of the United States teaches an ambivalent attitude toward vacations. You are told to study hard and work hard all year to save up for vacation time, but then when you go on vacation you are made to feel guilty for not being sufficiently workaholic. While on vacation, you will see students studying for exams and writing papers on their laptops and their parents checking in at work via their cell phone. I encourage you not to be one of these people and to fully enjoy the days you set aside for vacation.

Vacations need not be expensive. What you need is a change, a break from your everyday routine. You need to be renewed.

You will know you are renewed when you find you have new ways of looking at what had been a vexing problem prior to vacation. You will be able to put aside differences with your friends, realizing that all your angst was over a rather meaningless and trivial matter. You will come back to school with new energy and ready to take on new projects and leadership roles.

You may be surprised to find how refreshed your mind is. The book that you had so much trouble concentrating on before vacation now seems interesting and engaging. The coming semester's course load doesn't seem so daunting. The economics final that had you in a panic now seems like it didn't go as bad as you first imagined.

Vacations are not extra workdays. Take a break and enjoy yourself. It will help you be a stronger student.

100   Investigate Possible Career Choices

College is a good time to begin thinking seriously about career choices. As you explore the world of ideas, it's a time to find out about yourself, your likes and dislikes, your skills and challenges, and what kind of issues and tasks you find most stimulating. It's also a time to examine how you might fit best in the professional world of work.

It is not a good idea to think of your college education as career training. If you think of college as simply training for a profession, then you may get a good job credential from your college in the form of your diploma, but you will have missed out on a good college education. College is about learning and education. What you learn will no doubt be critical in whatever professional field you choose, but you should focus on learning as your priority.

How should you approach your career exploration? You should take a wide variety of courses to get an idea of where your interests lie.

You should participate in extracurricular activities to see how you like being involved in organizations and what activities hold your interest. You should do an internship or get a job in a field that carries some initial interest for you.

As you get more serious and focused about your studies, go to the career center or your department to find out how your academic interests line up and prepare you for different kinds of careers. You'll be surprised at how expansive your opportunities are regardless of your field of study. Every professional position will require you to be able to think critically, broadly, and innovatively. You will be called upon to do a wide range of tasks and to use a variety of skills in almost any field you choose. You may change careers more than once or twice, and you will certainly be required to retool and reconceptualize your work even in the unlikely event that you stay in the same career over a lifetime.

As you pursue a major, you will want to begin considering the opportunity to attend graduate and professional schools. You also may decide to go directly into the workforce. Be sure to keep all of your options open. While you may feel today that you can't conceive of attending school beyond your undergraduate degree, you may feel very differently as you enter your senior year of college. Similarly, going directly into the workforce after college is by no means an indication that you won't be entering a graduate program within a few years.

Those students who enter college with clear preprofessional goals, like business, law, medicine, and especially engineering, will have a much more defined curriculum right from the first year of college. While that training is important for your professional preparation, be careful to hold onto as much of the unique opportunity of a liberal arts education as you can. Take full advantage of your elective courses. Don't miss out on an undergraduate education because you are in such a hurry to advance professionally. You'll be working in that profession for the next forty or fifty years; your college education comes only once and for just a very few years in your lifetime.

A college education is essential for professional careers today. Do take advantage of your education to begin thinking about and preparing for your professional life. At the same time, don't be so focused on what's ahead that you don't allow yourself to fully experience and enjoy today the gift that a college education represents. You will find that your broad, liberal arts education will serve you well throughout your life and in every aspect of your career.

101 Remember Your College Accomplishments

You will have numerous accomplishments, large and small, during your college years. Be sure to make a note of them in a journal, in a file, in a video, or on your resume so that you can fondly remember these special moments and highlights of your college years. Time will go by so quickly that unless you have an intentional, organized system for keeping memories, you will lose track of so much good that you have done.

Some of your accomplishments will be in the academic arena. You may get comments from a professor expressing what an outstanding exam or paper you've written. Keep that paper and hold onto those special words. You may be more formally recognized by being placed on the college honor roll or acknowledged at a college honors ceremony. You might be invited to serve on a university policy committee or to give input into departmental curricular projects. You may win a prize for poetry, facilitate an interracial or interfaith dialogue, star in a theatrical performance, exhibit artwork, or be invited to attend a conference to talk about your research.

Other accomplishments will be based on your personal and community achievements. You might experience a new friendship or a first kiss—jot a note down about the experience. You may win a scholarship for civic involvement, be elected or appointed to a leadership position at Hillel or another organization, or get a promotion at your workplace. You might play in the school's marching band, make the varsity gymnastics team, or score the winning goal in an intramural game. Keep a file of all these accomplishments. Someone you admire may say something very complimentary about you—write in a journal how you felt.

If you're not the kind of person who keeps good files, then make sure you make good mental images of your accomplishments. First of all, be sure you accept the recognition you receive. You don't need to feel you're gloating to feel good about yourself. Try to hold onto the image of a compliment from someone you respect, a fun day with a good friend, or praise from one of your professors.

When you begin college, it will seem like you have an endless road ahead of you. You will soon find that your college days will go by very quickly. Hold onto your best memories, even as you continue to create special, new ones each and every day.